'THERE'S A WAR ON PET'

Boyhood Memories of County Durham

'THERE'S A WAR ON PET'

Boyhood Memories of County Durham
by Brian Joslin

ISBN 0 9522451 0 8

Film set in New Century Schoolbook, printed and bound by
Stanley L. Hunt (Printers) Ltd, Midland Road
Rushden, Northamptonshire

Published by B. Joslin Publications
The Gate House, Guilsborough, Northampton NN6 8PU
from whom copies may be obtained
Tel. (0604) 740229
Fax. (0604) 740713

ACKNOWLEDGEMENTS

I gratefully acknowledge the help and assistance given to me by the following:

Fellow authors, Dorothy Grimes and Edna Scott, for the benefit of their experiences in writing, for reading my draft manuscripts and offering constructive comments.

Anne Wright for her belief in this book, for deciphering and typing my handwritten scripts, and for her invaluable assistance with editing the text, through to its final form.

My wife Audrey and sons, Paul and Alistair, for their continuing encouragement and support with my writings.

There is no doubt that contemporary photographs bring the text to life and I am thankful for the loan of family snapshots from a number of friends.

Many photographs have been reproduced by kind permission of Beamish, The North of England Open Air Museum, County Durham, where Jim Lawson and his staff were so helpful with my researching into their photographic archive.

So many friends have given me encouragement, that it is impossible to name them all. I hope they will accept my grateful thanks.

Brian Joslin.

CONTENTS

FOREWORD

by Dr Frank Atkinson, OBE
Founder and Director of Beamish
The North of England Open Air Museum

The British working class way of life half a century ago is not well recorded "from the inside"; perhaps not surprisingly so, since the opportunity for a working class child to clamber securely into good education, and all that lay beyond, was uncommon. Hence the facility to record that way of life is rarely available and still more rarely utilised.

Brian Joslin has recalled his young War Years in Bishop Auckland, County Durham. This really is life: warts (and muck!) and all. Added to the ever-present difficulties of life near the edge of existence were the restrictions of wartime, as its title vividly reminds us.

One is reminded from time to time of sections in *The Uses of Literacy,* wherein Richard Hoggart (1957) recalled life in his Leeds pre-war working environment; descriptions of home life, of street life, of the corner shop: of Mam and Dad and going to tea at Grandma's; of hard times at school and smoking behind the fence.

Glimpses from *Kiddar's Luck* (1951) and *The Ampersand* (1954) may also relevantly occur to the reader. Jack Common, of Tyneside, recalled in these books his more urbanised environment, being born in a Newcastle suburb in 1903.

Brian Joslin's book is lively and readable and – so far as one can recollect oneself – precise in its sense of immediate recall. Its chapter headings such as "JOY AND SADNESS", "HAWKERS", "KIT AND CONKERS","SNOW AND MUCK", "CHAPEL", "BUMPS IN THE NIGHT" all lead to vivid stories and fascinating recollections.

The story ends as it begins, with the VE Day street party celebrations, and throughout records a vital part of a fast disappearing world, among a working-class community of County Durham during those years.

It provides another volume to be placed among that cherished shelf of such autobiographies: so many of them written in a "sweet and sour" realisation of what is now lost, but what has been gained from living through those experiences.

Frank Atkinson.

AUTHOR'S NOTE

In the hustle and bustle of life, childhood memories are often pushed into the far recesses of the mind. Although I had long thought of penning some of my early experiences, I never intended to write a book. But anyone who starts writing, will know that one memory triggers another to life. One by one, those little boxes begin to pop open, as if emerging into the sunlight from a dusty trunk of childhood memorabilia.

It was during a period of convalescence in hospital, following minor surgery in June 1992, that I first began to commit my reminiscences to paper. From earliest recollections of consciousness – the feel of the cold stone floor, the contrasting warmth of the clipping mats and the beckoning light shining through an open door to the outside world, bottled-up memories began to flow from my pen.

I trust that these random evocations have been successfully forged into a cohesive account of my young years. Some people's names have been changed, but not their personalities.

For those who lived through the war years in County Durham, I hope that my story will fan some embers of bygone times, into flames of nostalgia. And for the younger reader, allow a glimpse into a community and way of life, that despite everything, has not been replaced by anything better.

B.J.

To Audrey, Paul and Alistair

Harrowing at Mountjoy, Durham. April 1938

Grey towers of Durham
Yet well I love thy mixed and massive piles
Half church of God, half castle 'gainst the Scot
And long to roam those venerable aisles
With records stored of deeds long since forgot.

Sir Walter Scott (1771-1832)

CHAPTER 1

VICTORY

The tables were turned, the boot was now on the other foot and we had Adolf Hitler exactly where we wanted him. This evil beast who had terrorised the world for so many years, was well and truly defeated. He would now become the focus of our joy and merriment, that poor dejected figure, hanging by the neck from a hook on the water tower wall, paint brush in hand, awaiting the flames. VE Day had arrived at last, the culmination of our hasty preparations. As lads of ten and eleven years old, we had collected wood and old blackout shutters, anything that would make a good blaze and heaped it against the high wall. Only the older boys could remember Guy Fawkes nights, before the war, but this was going to beat any Gunpowder Plot bonfire, it would be much bigger and hotter and Hitler would have his just punishment.

Our effigy was made from a large white boilersuit out of somebody's jumble, which we stuffed with straw and rags. The head, with black button eyes, was a stuffed hessian sandbag complete with a black moustache. A wisp of black horsehair from a cushion swept forward over his brow beneath his steel helmet, a souvenir brought back by a released POW. This pathetic figure, with swastika armbands had been humped around the streets in a wheelbarrow tumbrel, to give everyone a chance to jeer and ridicule him before his execution. Meanwhile, our mams had been baking, making jelly and custard and sandwiches for the street party. Old bunting and flags from bygone victory celebrations were unfurled from fusty trunks and drawers, to dance and rejoice in sunlight once more.

There were no fairy lights that had survived the war years, but my dad had been resourceful in obtaining a string of lamp holders on a cable, which had been used as Christmas decorations outside a large department store before the war. This was long enough to stretch across the street from our bedroom window to the Dawsons opposite. My dad was in the electrical trade and had likewise obtained a box of coloured lamps of red, blue, green and yellow. He had borrowed some trestles, tables and forms from our Wesleyan Sunday School, which the wives had covered with white linen tablecloths. The neighbouring street had joined forces with ours, to organise the victory celebrations. Ladysmith Street, so named to commemorate another victory, when that South African town was relieved by the British, following a long siege, during the Boer War. This was a special holiday, no-one had to go to school or work, everything was going to be fine for us now, with no more fighting and bombing. I couldn't imagine what would be on the wireless at news time, with no war. How innocent and naive I was, in those heady days that led to victory.

At 3 o'clock in the afternoon, Mr Churchill spoke on the wireless and the tables were set for four o'clock. What a feast that was, mainly for us bairns. There was no exotic food, as strict rationing was in force, but there was tea and lemonade, jellies made from Ministry of Food orange juice or cherryade and gelatine. Meat paste, spam and egg and tomato sandwiches were piled high on plates. My mam had made a jam sponge cake, others had made apple pies and chocolate cakes with cocoa. A dozen pork pies were supplied by Mrs Pallister, a friend of my mams, with connections at the store bakery. The name Co-op was rarely used. This was a great novelty, a party in our street, we had never seen the likes before, everybody was happy and jolly with not a drop of strong drink in sight. The beverage was tea, gallons of it were drunk that afternoon. An extension loudspeaker into the street from our wireless set poured out music from its nail on the wall. Sergeant Dexter, our local bobby, was there from the next street, with his wife and Brenda who was about my age. He was laughing as only policemen can laugh, he'd forgotten the times when we'd raided his orchard, and we no longer tried to avoid him. The food was soon consumed, as our thoughts were one track and that was the bonfire. Everyone moved around the top house next to our school, to see the fire, which was already wet with paraffin and soon roaring like an inferno. How we all cheered and laughed with delight as the flames lapped around Hitler. He began to smoke, then burst into flames, oh what excitement, his face was burning and his steel helmet fell off into the fire. Soon he was beyond recognition and just a tattered smouldering rag hanging from a hook. We played around the bonfire for hours, poking and prodding until there was nothing left but a smouldering heap of glowing red ash. Some of us went home for large potatoes to roast by burying them in the hot embers. There was just a small bunch of lads left by dusk, the diehards, Carl, Arnie, Howard, Donnie and Jossie, that's me. We sat around the fire on milk crates from the school yard, waiting impatiently, probing with sticks, trying to hurry the roasting. Occasionally a handful of leaves and twigs would be thrown onto the fire by someone to make white smoke, then a burst of new flames. My eyes smarted and watered in the swirling smoke and the heat, but that was of no consequence. This was VE day, we had won the war. I felt so glad and happy. As I gazed at the glowing mass, I was mesmerised by the heat, the smell of fire, the drifting smoke and roasting taties.

My mind travelled back to my first recollections of being a conscious human being, back through the swirling mists of time to the place of my birth. I was weightless, levitating on the wings of my memory. I saw myself as a baby, creeping across a floor of cold stone flags. The cold flags contrasted with the warm clipping mats, that adorned the floors of all Durham coal miners' homes. Nobody in our family was posh enough to have a carpet, only cheap lino or 'canvas',

My door to the outside world

as my mam called it, laid on the floor. The flags were cold and smelled damp, as I moved, tortoise-like towards the beckoning light of an open door, which was my goal. A brass tap dripped into a galvanised pail of slops by the door. The water was cold, with a soap scum, which broke when I plunged my hand in to explore. This was the door to the outside world, with a flight of stone steps leading down to the ground, more common to a farm yard than human habitation. Crossing the threshold, I made for the steps. Looking downwards like a fledgling bird about to experiment with its wings, I moved towards the edge. I don't recall launching myself into space, but was told later that my mam had grabbed me by the rompers, in the nick of time. Later, I learned that this occurred at Aunty Mattie's house in High Potters Yard, near to our house. It was at 26 Front Street, Newbottle, Houghton-le-Spring, where I was born to Violet, née Lockhead and James Frederick Joslin, on a winter's day in 1935 under the sign of Pisces – the Fish.

The stone steps episode must have been around my first birthday as I was not walking and besides, we moved to Bishop Auckland when I was just over a year old. My dad had started in the pit when he left school at the age of fourteen. His father felt very pleased that young Freddie, was to be 'set on' at Houghton Colliery, as he had just lost his wife and desperately needed the extra money to try to make ends meet. Freddie had been the baby of the family and by all accounts a little weakling when he was first born. They would carry him about on a pillow for support, he was so weak. "Ar was just a little skeleton," my dad would relate, always the dramatic touch to enhance his tale. The doctor was in despair. "You could try giving him Virol," he advised his mother, "it will give him strength". A year or so later, the doctor was visiting my grandmother, she had never been well after her last baby. "My word," he exclaimed, "who's this bonnie little lass on the mat? What lovely curls". "Wi that's our Freddie, doctor", said his mam proudly. "We gave him Virol, as you suggested, and he's never looked back since". "How remarkable!, what a transformation!", exclaimed the doctor. "I'll make a point of writing to the manufacturers – they'll be pleased to hear, of such a success story".

So back to my tale. My dad having left school, went with his father to start work at six o'clock on the following morning as a wagon way lad, learning to lay and maintain the small gauge rail tracks used throughout the pit for transporting tubs of coal. My grandfather Josiah Joslin was known to be a good conscientious worker in the pit, a shifter, who could be relied upon. The colliery manager was pleased at the prospect of another good worker. Houghton Pit in the centre of the Durham coalfield, was the most unlikely place to find a Cockney. My grandfather was born in Whitechapel in the East End of London in 1860. Although this was a notorious slum area, his family were wheelwrights. The little I know of his background was gleaned from my dad. Josiah had lost his mother at the age of seven. It was not long before his father decided to re-marry and young Josiah was not wanted. A large Jewish family fostered the child, perhaps his name appealed to them. From the Bible they knew that Josiah had been the youngest King of Israel, being anointed King at the tender age of eight years. But this Josiah was to be no King. He was to be an unpaid servant, slaving long hours, carrying out chores. His last task at night, was to clean all of the family's boots before he was allowed to go to his bed.

At the age of thirteen, he got a job as a butcher's boy, delivering meat to wealthy houses in London, with a horse and cart. One day the horse bolted, Josiah was thrown into the cobbled road and the cart wheel ran over his foot. He suffered a broken toe and without any medical attention, he was to walk with a limp for the rest of his life. Fortunately, he was taken under the wing of the Christian Mission a group of people who were tackling the immense social problems in London. They were later to become known as the Salvation Army. Young Josiah received sustenance from the Salvation Army and was trained to become one of the first soldiers to fight their cause. He became a cadet and was later commissioned as a Lieutenant and posted to Torrington in Devon in 1885. Soon he was promoted to Captain and managed a food depot in London, serving the needy and destitute.

Cockney Boy in Durham

However, he had already fallen in love with a young lady, who was in domestic service in the Shaftesbury Institute. She was Emma Watson, from Rainton in County Durham, who had gone into domestic service in London, with her cousin Nelly. The outcome, was that Josiah resigned his commission, to marry Emma. This may have been because of the Salvation Army's strict rules, concerning the marriage of unequal ranks. Perhaps they took St Paul's words literally – "Be ye not unequally yoked", who knows? They rented a house in the Caledonian Road, where their first child was born, in 1891. I think Emma must have been homesick, for they moved to County Durham in 1892, where he got employment in the coalmines. An unusual change of direction for him, from soul winner, to coal winner. They raised a family of four girls and three boys, my dad being the baby of the family. Josiah always kept up his links with the Salvation Army and regularly attended the open air meetings where he played his concertina. One of my dad's brothers, Billy, became an engine driver and secretary of the local branch of the NUR. The eldest, Percy was a coal miner as well as being a talented artist. He would sometimes make sketches with chalk on pieces of canvas, which were used for ventilation screens in the pit. One day, whilst waiting at the bank head for the cage to take him underground to start his shift, young Percy made a quick sketch with a piece of chalk, on the wall. This was a caricature of the colliery manager, standing there with his lamp and stick. Just a bit of fun – he was a compulsive sketcher. A few days later, the colliery manager, who had seen his likeness, sent for Percy, to go to his office. It was with fear and trepidation that he approached the manager's office and feebly knocked on the door, "Ar'll surely be sacked", he thought. "Come in", called the manager, "Ah!, young Joslin, was it you that did that drawing on the bank head?" After a short hesitation the reply came, "Yes sir, Ar'm very sorry". "I thought it was very good lad, you should do something with such talent". Percy gave a sigh of relief. The outcome was that his shifts were arranged, so that he could attend evening classes at The Sunderland School of Art. Although uncle Percy worked in the mines all his life, he developed his artistic talent as a hobby and produced many fine drawings and paintings. In a later age he would have gone to college to study art, but that was not for the likes of him, he was a vital breadwinner and had to be content with his lot.

During my dad's years in the pit, in the twenties and thirties, he was brought face to face with death and tragedy on several occasions. There was little safety awareness in the mines in those days. Accidents were a regular part of pit life. The chilling sound of the colliery buzzer, would strike dread into the hearts of everyone for miles around. This was a signal that a man had been killed in the pit. Work was finished for that day and everyone came out-bye and to bank, and made their way home. The body would be brought home to his family, black from the pit, just as it had been recovered, for the family to deal with.

Shortly after the funeral, a brand new, wooden rollered mangle was delivered to the widow, with the compliments of the colliery company, so that she could take in washing to supplement her meagre pension. An insult you may think, but this was common practice in those days and accepted as an act of generosity. Fred was always interested in first aid and studied the subject in his spare time. He became a member of the St John Ambulance Brigade and won a medal of merit. One of his worst tasks was to help in the rescue of one of his pit marrers, who had been trapped by a fall of stone. Thomas Haines was fortunate to survive, but had both legs amputated by the rescue doctor, in order to save his life. Such was, and is, the price of coal.

My grandfather was very strict and narrow minded, which inevitably led to family rebellion. Although the girls attended the Salvation Army meetings, the two elder boys turned their backs on religion. Even though my dad became a Methodist and eventually a local preacher, he was accused of being a deserter by his father, which goes to show how narrow and constricted his views were.

It was the Harvest Festival at my dad's local Methodist Chapel at Sunnyside, near Houghton, that he first got his eye on a beautiful dark haired girl, with smiling Irish eyes, who had gone there with her sister. Her name was Violet Lockhead and they were smitten, although he was much too shy to approach this young lady at the time. Though my dad's sisters were still at home and looked after their father and brothers, some family had left home to be married and a smaller house with cheaper rent was needed. In due course the the family found a new house in Newbottle, a village on the hill, overlooking Houghton and only a mile or so away. After they moved house, my dad discovered to his great surprise and delight that Violet, his dream girl was a daughter of the family next door. Her mother had been widowed at thirty with two other daughters and a son. Violet's elder brother John, was a coal hewer, the dirtiest job in the pit. Her dad, William Lockhead had died in a mental institution following head injuries, caused by a roof fall in the pit. No compensation in those days just a small widow's pension. However the colliery management did provide her mother with the customary mangle, so that she could take in washing. She would also go potato picking in October, to help to make ends meet. My grandmother, was re-married about four years later, to Roger Elliott, also a coal miner. She had two daughters, Eva and Edith and a son Roger from her second marriage. Her husband however was a sick man as he had suffered a gas attack in the trenches of Flanders and had contracted tuberculosis. Despite several spells in a sanatorium, he died at the age of 45 years. So we had a situation, my grandmother with children of both marriages on a widow's pension. She was glad when they reached the age of fourteen and could start work to contribute to the family's budget. From the time of the move, my dad's fate was sealed, Violet and he started going out together. This however didn't go down well with Josiah who considered them a worldly family, token Church of England and, in his view, on their way to hell.

Josiah worked at the pit on permanent night shift, better paid no doubt. This had its problems as of course, as he was in bed during the daytime. Although a staunch Salvationist, he would sometimes lose his temper and let fly with some choice Cockney swear words, at noisy children who had disturbed his sleep. They knew what to expect if they woke Mr Joslin, the bedroom window would be thrust open and his head would appear to vent his wrath. He was a stern and joyless man by all accounts and local children were afraid of him, as he prophesied doom

Violet – Smiling Irish Eyes

Fred and Vi – Smitten

and damnation on them. How un-Christ-like. Perhaps he revelled in his life of self imposed penance, for deserting the ranks of the Lord. This was certainly my impression, when years later, as a small boy, I got to know him. A grumpy, miserable old man with a big chip on his shoulder. Never a kindly word, to me or my young sister, only, "Mind my toes," he would bark, if you got too near to him whilst playing. "Oh leave them alone dar" aunty Annie would say, "they're only bairns". She was my dad's sister and he lived in her home in those later years. Had to be kept in his place, they'd had enough of his domineering ways. Sometimes the sisters would be unkind, catty, winding him up, they would say when their dad got up for work, "Our Freddie was in next door again last night dar, mind you she's a canny lass is Violet". "He's going to hell" he would resound. "They're all bound for hell next door". You could say that he didn't bless the friendship. Needless to say, he wanted nothing to do with the wedding which took place in Houghton Parish Church in October 1932, during Houghton Feast. This was an annual event, with origins in the 16th Century. Bernard Gilpin, the Rector of Houghton, had been summoned to London to face charges of heresy, which carried the death penalty. Fortunately he broke his leg on his journey south and Queen Mary died before he was fit to travel. He returned to Houghton, to a great welcome and a holiday was declared. A service of dedication and a feast were held during the first week in October, which still take place today. He provided an ox for the people, to be roasted in the market place. This was a festive occasion and a time for weddings.

The newly weds had managed to rent the first floor of a terraced house in Newbottle, their first home. Jack and Ada Robson, who were friends, had also been married at the same time and they lived downstairs. By all accounts, Jack was a large and clumsy man, whereas Ada was pretty and petite. An unlikely match you may think, but in love, and so well suited to each other. There is a well known saying in the north on the subject of marriage partners, which has a ring of truth about it – "They pair themselves up better than God can pair them."

In those days a popular wedding present was household

items, especially crockery. My dad often related the tale about Jack and Ada, using away at their crockery collection and pushing all dirty plates under the sideboard until the weekend, when they would have one enormous washing up session, then repeat the process.

During the early years of marriage, my dad was still working down the pit and suffered from stomach pains, so much so, that he lost a lot of work and was sent to spend a few weeks at the NUM Convalescent Home at Connishead Priory, in Ulverston, Westmorland. His doctor hoped that the rest and convalescence would improve his health, as his problem could not be diagnosed with any certainty. Like most coal miners, his general health suffered due to the adverse working conditions, like working wet and breathing coal dust. The time was Autumn 1934 and my mam was 'great with child' – me. His stomach pains however did not subside with convalescence, but seemed to get worse. One evening, quite late, my dad complained to the nurse about the severe pains which prevented sleep and the matron was sent for. Matron was of the old school, she was a disciplinarian and stood for no nonsense. After giving Fred a quick examination, she concluded that he had been drinking too much – she knew Durham miners' reputation for knocking the beer back. Little did she know or understand that my dad was teetotal. A teetotal Durham pitman was a rare animal you might say. Early next morning, three of Fred's mates helped to get him dressed and slowly walked him into Ulverston, about two miles, to the Cottage Hospital. They knew he was desperate for help. He arrived in a state of collapse and was fortunate that there was a surgeon on duty. Peritonitis, was diagnosed, his life was in danger, only an immediate operation to remove his perforated appendix could save him.

His wife was sent for and a taxi was laid on to bring her over the Pennines, some ninety miles from County Durham. By the time she arrived that evening, Fred was sleeping off the anaesthetic. The operation had been a complete success. The matron of course had been informed and was beside herself with great concern at her complete misjudgment of the situation. She couldn't do enough for my mam and arranged accommodation for her in the nurses'

Fred with his mates – they saved his life

home, where she gave her a lot of fuss and attention. She even started knitting baby clothes for the expected new baby. Dad stayed on at the convalescent home for several weeks and made a good recovery. Whilst he was there, he was notified by the colliery management that his employment was terminated and that his free coal allocation would cease forthwith. This was a great worry to him, as the baby was soon due. It was only after pressure from the Union, that the mining company agreed to continue his weekly free coal allowance until he returned home. You can understand the bitterness generated by this heartless kind of treatment.

Jack downstairs, worked at the power station in Philadelphia, not far from Newbottle. He was a linesman's mate, on maintenance of the electricity supply network and was often called out in the middle of the night to go in to work. My dad said that Jack was the soundest sleeper he had ever known. Often when his boss came to call him to

Early days in Electricity Supply

work, it was Fred, being on the first floor who would open the bedroom window and had the task of rousing Jack by going downstairs and hammering on their bedroom door. By this means he got into conversation with Jack's boss and made it known that he wished that he had a job with the Electricity Company.

Not long afterwards, there was a vacancy and he was offered a job at the North Eastern Electric Supply Company, NESCO, based at the power station, but going out and about as part of a maintenance gang on the underground cable network. He had started as a 'third man', in a cable jointer's gang, repairing faults on underground cables and making new connections for people who were having the electric light installed.

The gang consisted of the cable jointer, mate and third man. His job was to get the hole out, by lifting paving flags and digging, to find the cables, lighting the coke brazier and generally carrying out labouring work. Not to mention filling in the hole and putting back the flags at the completion of the day's work. He learned a lot in those two years out of the pit.

There was great rejoicing when I finally arrived on the scene in that upstairs room, as it was over two years since the wedding and my mam was beginning to think that she perhaps couldn't have children, like Jack and Ada had discovered to their dismay. Jack asked if he could hold the new baby. This great big man had a heart of gold. After holding me for a few moments, he said, "Eeh Fred, tak' the bairn off us, Ar might crush him". A true and gentle giant of a man, what a shame that he was to be denied fatherhood, although they later adopted two children and gave them a loving home.

CHAPTER 2

BISHOP

Unfortunately the power station closed in 1936. However my dad had worked hard and progressed well. He was offered a promotion, the job of jointer's mate in Bishop Auckland, 'Bishop' for short, which was about twenty miles away, on the south western edge of the Durham coalfield. He lodged at first in a residential boarding house in Edward Street, but soon got his bearings and found a house to rent for his growing family. He always said, "Ar have a big wife and a little family to keep." My mother was always, 'that woman Ar live with'. Live with he did, until his death at the age of 82 years. These things were said in fun and made people laugh. They all laughed except my mam – she was the laughing stock.

He had been offered a nice house in Hexham Street just off Etherley Lane, by Joe Maloney, a retired boxer who had invested his winnings in the property market. The most unlikely real estate man you could imagine, a diminutive Rockerfeller, always smartly dressed. I remember seeing him in later years, often sitting on his hunkers on the grass verge outside the doctor's surgery. He had bad feet, which evidently hurt by the way he walked. Rather than sit on the benches in the waiting room, Joe preferred to have a fag outside until it was his turn to see the doctor.

Doctor Wardle's surgery was adjoining his home on Etherley lane. This large Victorian style house, set back from the road, had stables and a field for his horses. The surgery waiting room had originally been a conservatory and was painted dark green, with wooden benches around the perimeter. The floor was of cold red ceramic tiles. Nobody made conversation in the doctor's waiting room, they only sat staring into space, except when someone coughed, whereupon all heads would glance in that direction. A man would light a cigarette to clear his chest. Women never smoked in public. The smell of antiseptic and tobacco will never be forgotten. Grateful and relieved patients could be seen leaving, clutching their bottles of pink medicine, box of pills or salve.

Joe also had a fish and chip shop in Bishop, known to the locals as Smokey Joes. This was run by his wife, who had a sound business head and kept Joe in his 'plaice'. He did all the donkey work, peeling taties, chopping chips and preparing fish and batter. He never battered his wife though – she was gaffer. She took the money and gave change from her leather money bag that was always slung round her waist. She kept a tight rein on Joe, who I think liked a drop of booze now and again, when he could lay his hands on some money. Mrs Maloney was his guiding light and did a good job in keeping him on the straight and narrow. His nice clean white silk scarf was always neatly tucked into his jacket, but he never wore the traditional cloth cap on his neatly Brylcreamed and brushed, black hair.

Back to my tale. Joe was there to meet the removal lorry when Fred and Vi with their baby arrived at Hexham Street. A kindly man, "Hello bonnie lad, Ar've got another house Fred, which yer might like better, near the rec." My dad took the offer and the lorry trundled down to No 20 Hutchinson Street, to unload the few pieces of furniture that they had collected since they were married. I remember this as my first home and have fond memories of growing up there. The house had two bedrooms, a sitting room and scullery with a nice yard, coal house and lavatory. This was, our house. We were only a few doors off the rec, where there were swings, rings, a slide and a flat topped round-

Fred, proud as punch of his bairn

about called a teapot lid. My dad would take me there, as proud as punch of his bairn. The little garden at the front had a wall and a wooden gate but was only a little strip of soil, where my dad could grow a few flowers, but wide enough for a pram. Further down were the Browns with two boys Eric and Ronnie who were older than me. There were Langlands who delivered milk from a churn on a little hand cart and put it into a can or jug on your step. Later it was delivered in bottles with circular greased cardboard tops with a push out middle. With two of those your mam could make a pom-pom for your hat, out of spare wool.

Our front street had flagged pavements down each side. The road was made of hard stones for the horses to grip with plenty of free horse muck always available for the garden. I used to find studs from horses' hooves amongst the loose stones of the road, these were good for scratching on walls and paving flags.

After the Coronation of King George the Sixth in 1937, the new King and Queen came to Bishop Auckland. The streets were crowded as people waited for the Royal Car. Mam, dad and me were standing at the station end of Newgate Street, opposite Brotherton's Music shop. At first I was on my dad's shoulders and then he sat me on a high window ledge outside Brown's Sawmill, where I had a good view. There were great cheers as people waved their flags and I saw the King and Queen waving and smiling. The memory is so clear. I waved my flag as I gazed on them in wonder. Little did anyone guess that one day I would be presented to Queen Elizabeth The Queen Mother, as she became, and also to Princess Elizabeth, when she became the reigning monarch, in some place yet unknown to me, many miles from Bishop Auckland.

Our little street was the centre of my world before the war, sloping up towards the rec gates, there was no through traffic, nobody we knew had a car anyway. The only traffic was the store grocer, butcher, baker etc with their horses and carts. The coal man had a lorry that came once a week, but he used the back lanes where the coal houses were, at great inconvenience to housewives with washing hanging out.

Monday was washing day and my mam would start

early, boiling kettles and pans of water on the fire. On washing day, I knew to keep out of the way, as she set about performing her tasks of drudgery. We had a wooden barrel, open at the top, used for washing. This was our 'poss-tub', the forerunner of the washing machine, where washing was put into hot soapy water and possed relentlessly, with the other essential utensil, the poss stick. I always thought our poss stick was more like a tree trunk than a stick. It was of solid wood about four feet long and bleached white, with years of dunking in Oxydol. Like a giant rolling pin on its end, with a wooden handle crossing through it near the top. The business end, the bottom, was of much larger diameter, for pounding the washing.

Mam would seemingly stand there for hours in the back yard by the poss tub, lifting and dropping the poss stick, pummelling the washing with vigour, splashes of soap suds flying in all directions. We didn't have a wooden rollered mangle like most people, but had one of the latest rubber rollered wringers, which was clamped to the rim of the tub. Batches of washing were processed and then she would put them through the wringer, one hand lifting and feeding washing into the rollers and the other turning the handle with her great bare arm, and the strength of Pansy Potter, the strong man's daughter, in the Beano. Sometimes she would let me have a poss or let me feed the washing into the wringer. When all had been washed, then the rinsing with fresh cold water, Reckitts Blue for the whites and further wringing, before hanging out to dry in the back lane. Out went the clothes line, zig-zagging between hooks on the brick walls. Regardless of the weather, my mam always had bare arms and I can still picture her pegging out the washing, with rosy cheeks, rosy arms and wind-blown dark hair, worn in a roll.

When it was raining all of this activity went on in the scullery and kitchen. The weather was never used as an excuse. There was a four railed wooden clothes line suspended from the kitchen ceiling, just in front of the fireplace. This was on pulleys so that it could be lowered down. Usually sheets and bedclothes were hung on this line before it was hoisted on high, like a mainsail, to dry. Smaller items were hung on a large clothes horse that was placed in front of the fire or on a clothes line across the scullery. There is nothing to equal the smell of clean wet washing, hanging about in the kitchen, a smell unknown to today's generation, but part of the rich texture of life in those days. Then there was my dad's dinner to get ready, with saucepans on the fire or chip pan on the gas ring. He would be tired when he came home from a hard day's work. By the look on his face sometimes, he must have felt as tearful as the streaming window panes, as he ducked under the washing with a grouse or two.

Inevitably, Tuesday was ironing day, with its own very distinctive clean smell. My mam had one of the latest electric irons, which she plugged into the light, with a two-way adaptor. She would check if it was hot enough, by licking her finger and touching the iron, to make it hiss. The light bulb and dangling flex would swing merrily from side to side as she slid the hot iron back and forth along the creaking wooden ironing board. Having taken all the trouble of getting the washing dry, I would be puzzled at her sprinkling water on things before ironing. "Why do you wet them again mam"? I would enquire. "Oh that's to get the wrinkles out and make everything nice and smooth". I remained puzzled.

Nobody seemed to know when the coal man was coming, but it was always on someone's washing day. "Oh here's Barker" the wives would exclaim, when they had just pegged out the last sheet. These were Durham girls and rarely complained at the inconvenience. "Never mind, we'll soon get the lines out again when he's gone, we have to have our coals". "Its a canny day pet. Do you want any coals?" said the ever cheerful and grinning black faced Mr Barker, with flashing white teeth, like Al Jolson. His dirty cap was always on the skew and he wore an armless leather jerkin over his grimy jacket to cushion his back against the lumpy bags. The inevitable leather money bag was slung about his shoulder from a leather strap, bandolier fashion. He fitted the part, a coal man through and through, with his alsatian dog standing four-square on top of the cab, as always. I think Rex enjoyed that elevated and superior position, where he could peer into back yards at other dogs and be at least level with the cats on the coalhouse roofs. The wives were always cheerful, "Bah!, you always pick my wash'n day". There was no apparent planning of coal deliveries, they just happened.

Sometimes when my mam was caught unawares, without any money, she would tell me to, "Keep down and hide. He'll put me a bag in and Ar'll pay him next week." Someone once complained that they had been given short measure. Mr Barker was indignant at the very thought that he should be accused of dishonesty. "Ar've never done that in my life" said he, with hurt pride, as his red nose grew longer by the second from his black face, just like Pinnochio's. We never suffered delivery shortages in our street as everyone could count to two. Hand to mouth they called it, at a shilling a hundredweight. Anyway posh folks who had a ton, or half a ton wouldn't miss the odd bag. No doubt it helped to keep his dog in bones. So much for the coal man.

The chimney sweep was more considerate, he swept before eight in the morning. Mr Donovan came in response to a request sent via his lad at the school – a little note. "Can you please sweep my chimney next Monday morning"? – he usually arrived already black from night shift at the pit, to execute with great skill, his part time job. "Bah!, he never leaves a speck of soot" the wives would say, "well worth sixpence". He would leave the soot in a sack for your allotment if you wanted, good for your plants, natural and better than slug pellets, which were then unknown. His bairn was called Donald or Ducky, a useful messenger before the telephone. An old Morris Ten was used to transport equipment and soot, no-one else we knew had a car. He must have worked very hard and saved to buy this.

Over the other side of the street, in my little world, were the Neashams. Tommy was a blacksmith at the store. Short and broad with immense muscular arms, usually sporting a pipe and a buoyant grin. When I was older I would spend many an hour watching him at work, plying his craft in the blacksmith's shop, not far from us.

Next door down from Neashams was Mr Gowton, who I always thought of as a very old man as he stooped and walked very slowly, with the aid of a stick. He had silver hair with matching bushy eyebrows under the peak of his cloth cap, which he wore always, even in the house. I never saw him without his cap and wondered if he wore it in bed. A pleasant and kindly man, especially to bairns. He would reach into his pocket and give me a penny when I ran ahead of him to hold open the rec gate. "There yer are bonny lad," he would smile, and pat my curly head. Sometimes I would go with him to the first bench in the rec, where he would meet up with other old men, for a smoke and a bit crack.

Now he was a pipe smoker and a habitual spitter. In the house he used the fire, which made a hiss, the done thing indoors. When I told my mam, she was disgusted. "You should only spit out orange pips," she proclaimed, that was acceptable. But she made my dad spit blood at times, not pips. Mr Gowton always smoked Warhorse and as my dad was a non-smoker, the ritual fascinated me as a small boy. His baccy was unwrapped from silver paper, a solid black block. "D'yer see that knife pet," he would say, as he produced an ancient horn handled penknife from his jacket pocket. "Ar've had that knife fotty year, right through France int' Great War." The blade was worn to a thin and shiny point, with use. "That's cut a canny bit baccy in them years," he boasted, as he began to pare away at the block, producing thin slivers of tobacco. Then the rubbing between palms, calloused with a lifetime of manual work. The process was slow and deliberate, as he cracked away to his mates on the bench. As a four year old, I would try to imagine how long forty years was. It must have been in the olden days. Then the ritual loading of the pipe and stoking up. Striking a match, puffing. How he didn't burn his fingers mystified me, as he would hold out the dying match by the curled black end for me to blow out. To this day the smell of pipe tobacco always reminds me of Mr Gowton, sitting puffing plumes of white smoke into the sunlight, and spitting on the ground. His housekeeper, Mrs Belshaw, was an old lady, who always wore a neat pinnie and a mop cap. I recall venturing into their house, into their sitting room. She beckoned me, "Come and see what Ar have in this drawer," as she slid it open. I stood on my tiptoes to peer inside, expecting a nice surprise. There was a rolled up leather belt. "You see that. It's a strap for naughty boys." I felt frightened and knew what to expect if I misbehaved in her house. What I'd done to warrant her warning, I can't imagine, perhaps she knew from experience, that little boys were as likely as not, to be naughty! She used an expression that was foreign to me, 'wi'not' and would say "Bah, they wi'not get me down that street, till this snow's gone." I thought it strange, a country expression, not native of Bishop. Further down the other side of the street was Mrs Graham who had a lodger with a big moustache and a raincoat. He was the first man I ever saw with a rolled umbrella, which he used as a walking stick. My dad said, "Ar think that man's a bit of a Nancy." This puzzled me, as to why a man with an umbrella should have a woman's name.

Holdens' Bazaar was just opposite Wesley Chapel and built on a slope. It was down hill from the front door to the far end of that long narrow store. Similar to Woolworths in some ways, yet so different in others. Dark, mysterious, tinkling, like an Aladdin's cave of treasure. With all manner of toys, dolls, puppets, brightly coloured Chinese lanterns, baubles and beads, paper masks and balloons, hanging from the walls and ceiling. To me, this was a world of magic, a world of tinsel and of Christmas – mind boggling. The proprietor, old Mr Holden, clad in his long flowing smock and a purple velvet smoking cap would seemingly float around, silently, all-seeing, all-hearing, all-knowing with his wisping white whiskers. Like a mandarin, inscrutable as his smile. He missed nothing! My mam had taken me there one morning whilst she was out shopping, just to have a look around. Roaming loose, I gravitated to the end of the store, gazing around, lost in wonder, mesmerised by the sights and sounds, trying to take it all in. Suddenly, there was a sharp tap on my shoulder – the spell was broken.

As I turned around, there was a hideous monster, towering over me with the grotesque face of a witch, with hooked nose, pointed chin and bulging eyes. She began to laugh at my sudden terror. "Wi it's only me," assured Mrs Belshaw as she removed the mask. She was standing next to my mam. This was her idea of fun, but it gave me nightmares. I was never more pleased to clasp hold of my mam's hand.

Enough of Mrs Belshaw and her mask, which on reflection was more beautiful than her natural face – especially when she pointed to the strap.

Auckland Castle, just off the market place, had been the seat of the Bishops of Durham since the twelfth century and the hundreds of acres of parkland were always open to the public. There was a magnificent deer house and shelter near the castle, but the days were long gone, when the ruling Prince Bishop hunted deer and wild boar in his oakland, with his noblemen. I recall my mam taking me into the Bishop's Park for a picnic. We never saw the Bishop, he stayed in his castle. I think his boss Jesus would have greeted everyone who came into his park. Did Jesus hunt deer? – I thought he made them. I'm getting too philosophical for a four year old, never had such thoughts then. My mam made lovely banana and egg and tomato sandwiches, which we had with our picnic in the park, by the deer house. There were no more bananas to be had after that. She told me, "They've all gone from the shops, there's a war on pet". That explained a lot of the changes taking place in my little world. When I tasted bananas again after the war, I recalled the deer house and that wonderful picnic.

Entrance Gateway to the Bishop's Park

CHAPTER 3

TRAVELS

Sometimes during the summer before the war, we would go
to the seaside for the day, to Roker. Preparations started
early in the morning as the excitement built up. Eggs,
boiled the night before, were shelled and mashed up in a
basin with skinned tomatoes. Loaves of bread were sliced
and buttered. This home made spread was laid on liberally,
salted and peppered – the sand was added later! Then
there were bananas to mash with a fork with added sugar
and cream from the top of the milk. Before long there
would be piles of sandwiches, neatly wrapped in greaseproof paper stacked on the kitchen table. Teacakes were
sliced and buttered and filled with strawberry jam. Home
made spiced loaf, my dad's favourite, was always included,
just called, spice. "Bah Vi," dad would remark as he viewed
the mountain of food, "you'd think you were feedin' the five
thousand. We'll never eat all this." My mam always rose to
the bait. "Wi don't forget there'll be a nation of folks there,
there's not just us you know. There's our Mattie and Jack
and me mother, then there's the bairns. And you know
what that Roker air does to your appetite!"

Before the war, we always met up with my gram-ma,
cousins, uncles and aunts who also brought their picnics.
As you would expect, we were never known to be short of

The Durham train approaching Bishop Station

eats. Off we would go fully laden to the station to catch the Sunderland train. My dad would get the tickets at a little window, then we would await the arrival of the train, on that grimy, draughty platform. There was a scruffy little porter who was always bustling about, known as Allswap. This was the word which he would bellow at the top of his voice, for people to change trains. My mam couldn't stand him, always swearing. It was always a great thrill to go puffing out of Bishop, through the tunnel under Bondgate and then on to the viaduct across the Wear valley. On we would steam, through Brancepeth and Durham City, Fence Houses and onwards, towards Sunderland and the sea.

Once outside Sunderland station, we would walk a little way to the tram stop. Me with bucket and spade and my mam with a big bag. My dad would have his shirt neck open, in sporting mood and would perhaps take his jacket off, if it was warm. The tramcar stop was not far away. The trams came and went every few minutes. He would say,

"Brian, look out for trams that say Roker". There were some trams that said Roker via Fulwell, which really confused me. Anyway, we got on the Roker tram, with the other folks that were waiting and perched ourselves on the wooden slatted seats. 'Ding ding' and we were off. To me, this was an enchanted journey with the whine of the motor, the smell of the tram, the driver always standing, not like on a bus, I wondered why, and still do. The conductor would appear with his ticket machine. "Move down the car now" he would call.

Clang, clang, clang, as we crossed the points. Somebody pulled the cord that ran along the ceiling when they wanted to get off, ding went the bell. Then a squeak of breaks would bring us shuddering to a halt. What a magical bumpy, ride. Then my dad would say "Look Brian we're coming to the Wear bridge". This mighty structure spanning the river, was in my eyes, awesome to behold, green and large, with lots of steel and rows of rivet heads. Then we would pass Roker Park, the home of the famous Sunderland football team. My mam would announce proudly, "That's where Bobby Gurney plays". He was a relative of my mam's, and a legendary centre forward for Sunderland, being instrumental in them winning the 1937 FA Cup at Wembley, the first Cup Final ever, to be televised. Many faithful supporters, made the trip on special excursions, even though they had no hope of getting into the match. Hundreds crowded round London shop windows, to capture the fever of that great day, from those tiny snowy screens.

Soon, we rounded a bend and the sea was in view. There were a number of large houses with gardens which faced the sea at Roker. These belonged to wealthy families, usually in shipping or shipbuilding. "That's the house where Ar was in service", my mam would say as she pointed out where she had worked as a housemaid and cook, starting at the age of fourteen on leaving school. Boys went into the pit and girls into service, with few exceptions. She used to tell, how her mother had got her fixed up with this job, in response to an advertisement in the Sunderland Echo. "Me mother took me to be interviewed to this big house in Roker. She did all the talking mind you. Told them Ar was used to housework which was true enough, and that Ar was a 'beautiful cook'. This was a bit of a fib, we never had anything much to cook. Anyway, Ar got the job and learned as Ar went along. The wages were 4/6d a week and no callers. On me one day off a fortnight, Ar could go home. Mind you, Ar had me bed and board. The mistress always gave me a new white cap and pinnie, for Christmas. Eeh!, she was kind to us, she would give us cakes and treats to take home for the younger bairns in the family." Her employer, was a ship-owner who was very strict, but fair, in his dealings with the servants. He was always addressed as, The Master.

At last we would disembark on the sea front and make our way down the Cat and Dog Steps, which zig-zagged down to the beach, near Roker pier. Sure enough, we would soon see some well known faces and settle down with deck chairs. If it looked like rain, which seemed quite often, my dad would hire a beach tent for the day. This was tall, with

Roker Tram

a flat top and was soon erected on its wood frame. Then we would shovel sand into the canvas pockets around the bottom, until they bulged. Out would come our little meths stove, just a little round tin with holes in the side and the tin kettle was soon on, for cups of tea all round.

The sea was beckoning and us bairns couldn't wait to get our cossies on. These had been knitted by our mams, with straps and little legs. Fine until the moths got in. Then off we would rush down to the sea to go plodging. Alan, my cousin would say, "Howay Brian, are yer comin' for a plodge", and off we would go. That first contact with the North Sea, had to be experienced to be believed. Notoriously cold, even at the height of summer. A few quick wincing steps, then out again quick. "Ooh", we would shout as we did a war dance on the sand, before venturing back for another go. Gradually we became accustomed to the sea, as our legs turned blue. After that initiation, we were fine and would have lots of fun. My dad would venture in, socks off and trouser legs rolled up. We would hold hands and walk into the waves. He would dance about with the initial shock. "Ooh, mother, yer bairns is on fire", he would shout, which seemed to have an anaesthetic effect, as he would laugh, repeating, each time he ventured back in. When we'd had enough, back we would head to our tent and cluster of deck chairs. "Bah, you look starved" my mam would say, "come and have a nice rub down, with this towel and get warmed. Yer'd better have yer vests on, Ar don't want yer catchin' cold." Then I would begin to feel cosy, the blood would begin to circulate once more and my legs would lose their blueness.

Our primeval urge to make contact with the sea, had once more been satisfied, it had all been worthwhile, to feel so cosy now. "Bah!", my dad would sometimes say, "that sand's warm", as he slumped back into his deckchair and buried his aching feet. "It's just like banging yer head against a brick wall. Lovely when yer stop". Then everyone would have a good laugh. Our family were good laughers, knew how to enjoy themselves. "Come on Alan, come on Brian, do yer want a sandwich" gram-ma would say. Those sandwiches were delicious, there's nothing like a plodge in the North Sea to whet your appetite. It seemed to always

*Roker Sands with Roger, Mam and Alan – not forgetting
the donkey and me*

be breezy and sand got everywhere. That unmistakable
crunch, in the egg and tomato sandwiches was an essential
part of a seaside picnic and never-to-be-forgotten.

Then there would be a ride on the donkeys, a great
adventure along the sands and back. Then the building of
sand castles and making pot pies. The sand had to be
slightly moist for pot pies and castles to hold together. You
would fill your bucket with sand, turn it over quickly,
before the sand fell out, then pat the underside of your
bucket with your spade and chant to the beat. "Pot pie
daisy, my mother's lazy". Only then could you be sure that
your pot pie had set. It always worked. "Bah, Ar'll catch
you, yer little monkey" my mam would shout in mock
anger. Then we would all laugh again.

Castles built and pot pies set all about, we would look for
further amusement. My dad would say, "Come on you lads,
Ar'll take yer to see Holey Rock, now the tide's gone out a

bit," and off we would go with him along the beach. This was a well known rock headland at that time, jutting out onto the beach and so named because it was riddled with caves and passages, pummelled out by the sea. It was a great thrill to go into the rock and explore. Over the years there had been people trapped in there by the incoming tide, so my dad said and they had drowned. For that reason, part of the rock had been blasted away, but it was still exciting. We would then go onto the rocks, looking for crabs and fish in the pools. As always, we would find a nice piece of seaweed to take back home. This would be hung on a nail in the back yard to tell you when it was going to rain. Back at our tent, there was a man coming round with tripod and camera, taking snapshots which were produced in a few minutes for sixpence and so we would sit and pose. The results were rather disappointing, dark brown, like night time, but what could you expect for a sixpenny instant picture?

There were always some roundabouts and side shows near the pier, which we would visit. Our favourite ride, as lads, was on the swing boats, always called shuggie boats. There's nothing to beat a good shuggie. Once you got into your seats facing each other, the idea was to take the opposite rope from above, to be pulled in turn. Then the excitement began, first with a gentle swinging, to and fro, gradually working up into a great arc. You would sometimes think you were going over the top, when you nearly left your seat, before plunging earthward again, with a whoosh of wind past your ears.

Our shrieks of delight added to the rich cacophony of sound in that small fairground. The Dutch organ, with blurting pipes, banging drums and clashing cymbals. The man turning a big wheel that reminded me of a gigantic washing mangle, driving the roundabout and shouting, "Howay now hinnies, get ya tickets for the roondaboot, penny a torn, penny a torn." Then repeating like a cracked record. My dad would let us have a go on the hoop-la, but not on the 'Win All' machines, that devoured your pennies and ha'pennies, in promise of rich rewards. That was gambling and "The start of the slippery road to ruin," so my dad said. Rain would send us scurrying back to escape the downpour. This was no hardship, but only created more fun and laughter. The flat top of the tent must have been designed to catch water as it filled into a great sagging pool. "Ar hope it doesn't burst," my dad would joke, "or we'll all get drownded," to more laughter. When the rain stopped, we emerged, to repair our castle and have some more sandwiches. By the end of the afternoon, we would gather up all our belongings and trudge back across the beach, to the Cat and Dog Steps and the trams, towards home. We couldn't wait for the next trip to Roker.

As a local preacher, my dad would travel around the circuit to all the different chapels to conduct the service and consequently became well known in the Bishop area. He was a popular preacher, especially for Sunday School Anniversaries. There would always be a children's story in the morning or afternoon service and he knew how to tell them. Preparation was the key to his success as a preacher and his sermons were always interesting, full of quips and humorous quotes, windows, he called them. These windows allowed the light to shine through and used to good effect to get the Gospel message across. One of dad's favourite villages to visit was Lands. This was well out into the country and not easy to reach. The nearest bus stop was a mile or so from the village and ordinary working folk had no motorcars in those days, only the bus, the train or shanks' pony.

His first appointment at Lands Chapel was shortly after we moved to Bishop and he would often relate his experience. Having been directed to get the OK bus from Bishop to Cockfield, the minister had said, "Just ask the conductor to let you off at Esperley Lane End, then take the lane signposted Lands. After a good mile, you will come to a long row of houses, this is Lands. The first house is God's House, the chapel. At the second house, first in the row, is the home of Mr and Mrs Branch and Tommy will be sitting on the step smoking his pipe. This is where you will go for your tea". Tommy was a retired railway worker and my dad was always made to feel at home there. Their son Roy, lived next door with his wife Celia. They kept hens for a living and raised their own flock.

I must have been about four when my mam and dad took

me to Lands to visit the Branch family. An unforgetable experience for a small boy, this was like going to another country, with different customs. The people were all very kind and friendly, they couldn't do enough to make you feel at home. What a great adventure it was for me to go there. Old Mr and Mrs Branch had invited us one Saturday and we were to go to see the hens and stay for tea. The walk from the bus stop was no problem, as my dad carried me on his shoulder for most of the way. From my vantage point, I could survey the countryside as we plodded on towards our destination. There were some pit heaps from the local colliery which towered away at the side of the lane, as we went down into a dip to cross the railway line. This was the line which linked Bishop with the Pennines and beyond. Then we climbed a steep and winding road towards the village, which soon came into sight. "Look, you can see the chapel now", as the largest building for miles came into view. "Now look over there in the fields," my dad said, "d'yer see all those huts, they're all Roy's hens".

There were large wooden hen houses, scattered at random across a field and I could soon hear the cry of the roosters, as they strutted about amongst the clucking hens. We approached the houses. As sure as eggs was eggs, there was this little old man smoking his pipe, on his front step, as predicted. Mr Branch was just as my dad had described him. "This is Vi and our Brian, he's been looking forward to seeing the hens". He pushed his cap back, took his pipe out of his mouth and beamed a great smile. "Howay in, yer must be ready for a sup tea. Our lass has put't kettle on". The weather was autumnal and it was nice to see a welcoming coal fire with a singing black kettle on the hob. Mrs Branch was a pleasant little body, with a pasty white face, wearing a white apron over her dress and her grey hair tied in a neat bun. "Hello Fred, Ar'm glad yer've brought Mrs Joslin and t'bairn. Have you had a good journey? Hello Brian, bah, what lovely curls. Now come on up tit fire and get warmed". I gazed round and took all in. The range was freshly black leaded, with a shining brass fender, everything was spick and span. The floor was wood boards with lovely clipping mats. There was a smell of paraffin and pipe tobacco, which reminded me of Mr Gowton in our

street. The smell of newly baked bread and apple pies drifted across from the wooden kitchen table, where they had
been put to cool. A tabby cat was curled on a chair. "When
we've had a sup tea, Ar'll tak yer to see't 'ens Brian, would
you like to come an'all missus, we'll find some new laid
eggs for yer to tak back 'ome." I was a little puzzled by the
country accent, but soon learned to understand. "So long as
yer have no cows", said my mam, who was terrified at the
very thought. "Wi no pet" assured Mr Branch, "there's nee
beast 'round 'ere, only 'ens. Mind you we 'ave two tame
nanny goats, but nowt to worry about". Mrs Branch's idea
of a pot of tea was unlike anything we had been used to, it
was very strong, dark brown, even with milk. My mam was
a great one for putting her foot in it, as they say. She
would think aloud, "We just like our tea weak". "Oh, leave
it be a bit, let it draw, yer don't want to be suppin' watter",
replied Mrs Branch. When the tea was drawn, to her satisfaction, it was poured. "Bah! that looks strong", came the
expected response, "it'll be too strong for our Brian". I eyed
the dark brown fluid with suspicion and whispered to my
mam. I was very shy and always afraid to speak out.
"What's he say 'oney?" interrupted Mr Branch. "Could he
have a drink of water"? His reply, was memorable, a classic
to be handed down in our family, to yet unborn generations. "Wi course 'e can. 'Ere, tak this pot, there's plenty
watter in't tap". My mam took me into the damp smelling
whitewashed scullery and sure enough there was a tap,
sticking from a pipe on the wall, no sink! This was different to our water at home, it looked like very weak tea and
had a lovely fresh taste. "Bah, the water's brown,"
remarked my mam. "Yes 'oney, it's peat yer knar, puts 'airs
on yer toe nails," laughed Mr Branch.

When we'd had our drink, Mr Branch put his cap on and
jacket, "Howi then, we'll gan ower't 'ens". We followed him
out. "Ar'll just give our Roy a shout", at that he lifted Roy's
sneck. "We've got Fred an them 'ere, Ar'm just takin' them
owert' ens". Roy appeared, with a great beaming smile. A
younger version of his dad, only taller. "Howi in to see
Celia" and we all filed in. "Seest tha Celia, we's 'ere. Fred
wit' wife an' bairn". Celia was a perfect match in size for
Roy. Bespectacled, she had short cropped hair and wore a

beaming smile. "Bah, it's nice to see yer. Howay Monty, do yer want to gan tit 'ens". At this a small terrier appeared from under the table, furiously wagging his tail, this was, Our Monty.

Off we trooped across the road and through a gate towards this ramshackle farm building. This was a store and brooder house, where chickens were hatched by broody hens, known as clockers. So called because of the clock, clock, clock noises they made as they sat on batches of eggs, that they rarely left until hatched. In the next room there was a shallow wooden tray, with a dozen or so cheeping chicks. They were covered in a beautiful yellow down and were only two days old. I looked on in wonder and amazement, at these little creatures as they scratched about, picking up food under a powerful paraffin lamp that hung on a chain from a beam. "Yer've got to keep them warm Fred yer knar, 'specially in't first few days" said Roy, as he pumped the lamp. "These are all Rhode Island Reds, good layers an' good for't pot." Then we went with Roy on his rounds. There were six large wooden sheds, spread about his large field, each with its own population of hens, which must have numbered hundreds. As it was daytime they spent their time scratching about the field, only going inside when they wanted to lay an egg in one of their nests. There was a continuous chorus of hen chatter, clucking and clocking, with the occasional call of a cock bird – just to prove that he was there. There was a long felt covered hinged lid at the end of the first shed, over the nest boxes. Roy lifted the lid and secured it open with a piece of wood. Sure enough there were the nests of straw, two with hens sitting, others had clusters of brown, warm eggs with the occasional white pot egg. These were left there to suggest a laying place to the less experienced hens or those that had a tendency to, lay away, out in the long grass somewhere. "Howay," Roy invited, "would yer like to put't eggs into this pail". Mam helped me, and by the time we had been around all the nests, the pail was full and piled high with beautiful new laid eggs. There was one egg that had no shell, just a soft sack. Roy explained that that hen must be short of grit which was essential to make good shells. "Ar'd better fill that grit box tomorrer", remarked Roy as we

Roy with his hens

headed back to our tea.

Mrs Branch had been stoking up the fire for our return, which was a welcome sight when we entered their little house. We all enjoyed our tea of freshly baked bread with butter and jam and bramble and apple pie. I noticed that beside their sideboard, they had, what I thought was a tall wardrobe with a drawer at the bottom. Mr Branch was very pleased and proud to demonstrate their folding bed. "What'yer think o'this". We had never seen the likes, he just opened the doors and pulled down a bed on hinges, ready for the surprise guest. He said, "see, if yer mis't last bus, we can put yer up in our Chiffonier Bed," to roars of laughter. The bed was soon folded up out of sight as quickly as it appeared, as I looked on in wonder and amazement.

As it was getting dark, the oil lamp was lit and hung from a hook on the ceiling. This soon gave a warm glow to

the room with an unforgettable smell of paraffin. I recall
that scene to this day when I catch the smell of a paraffin
lamp. A trip to their lavatory was an adventure in itself.
One of a row of earth closets across their back way.
"There's a box o' matches and a candle on't seat. Blow it
out when yer've done and don't fall down't 'ole," Mr Branch
laughed.

We soon had to say goodbye and made our way back to
the bus by torchlight, mam's bag laden with eggs. We had
allowed plenty of time to spare, but my secret wish was to
miss the bus and sleep in that folding bed. What a memorable adventure – never-to-be-forgotten, that first trip to
Lands.

CHAPTER 4

JOY AND SADNESS

Christmas was a time of wonder and magic in those years before and during the war and Santa Claus was very much in mind. He was, to me, a high and mighty person, like God or the doctor, to be held in awe. My mam had taken me into the store drapery department in Bishop, just before Christmas. There was a massive staircase to the next floor, from the end of the drapery department. "Look Brian", she pointed, "there's Santa". She might have said "There's God", for I was rooted to the spot with fear, at this great rosy faced white bearded figure with his red cloak, white fur trimmed hood and big black boots. He beckoned me to come up to him. Alas I was not yet prepared to meet my maker and clutched onto mam with sobs and tears. "He's shy" she said and headed towards the door and home with me. That episode gave me nightmares, coming so near to Santa, my future contact would always be by letters sent up the chimney – much safer.

The approach of Christmas was heralded by a stream of carol singers who started to appear in early December, with knocks on the door in the evening. Groups, usually boys, would sing 'Good King Wenslas' or 'While Shepherds Watched'. My mam would always give them a penny, unless there were too many in succession, when she would shout, "Yer're too late, we've had carol singers already tonight". This caused immediate silence. I never went carol singing before the war, I was too young, but did often during the war and later and 'first footing' on the morning of New Years Day to make pocket money. The shops like Woolworths and Holdens took on a new image in the weeks leading up to Christmas, with Christmas trees, sparkling decorations, balloons and toys. At that time, Woolworths boasted that they sold nothing more expensive than sixpence, the name above the shop said: FW WOOLWORTH 3d and 6d STORES. Pocket knives and fountain pens were much wanted presents for Christmas. Other favourites were nurses' uniforms for girls, bus conductors' outfits for boys, complete with ticket punching machine which went ding, when you punched a ticket. Woolworths had axes, that I would gaze at with longing. My greatest wish was to have an axe for Christmas, so that I could go out chopping trees or railings. Despite asking Santa Claus, I never did get an axe for Christmas and wondered why? The presents were always exciting and the thrill of going downstairs on Christmas morning will never be forgotten. I think I was four years old when I got a tricyle or 'Fairy Cycle' as they

Tring-a-linging about in the back lane on our Fairy Cycles

were called. My friend Eileen, also had one the same Christmas. These were probably secondhand tricycles, that our dads had renovated, but to me it was sparkling and brand new, with a shining bell, to go tring-a-ling-a-linging about in our back street, with my pals.

On Christmas Eve we would all hang up our stockings from the shining brass rail under the mantle piece. Labels were fixed onto each stocking with large safety pins, MAM, DAD and BRIAN. The year of the Fairy Cycle was exceptional and a very expensive present that my parents must have saved for, or if it was new, had probably bought it with a Doggarts Club. This was a large departmental store in the market place, that sold a great variety of goods. Credits of £5 or £10, were entered into your club book, which was then paid off at a shilling a week, to the Doggarts Club Man who called, with his little book and pencil. The store ran a similar scheme and most working class families used this to purchase expensive items.

The black shining kitchen range was specially black leaded for Christmas, as it was every Saturday night in preparation for Sunday. The steel fender was polished like silver. There was a fringe with tassels that was fixed to the wooden mantle piece with drawing pins. On the mantel piece there were some ornaments and a tin tea caddy with pictures of the King and Queen. This was where my mam kept money for housekeeping.

She would plan to finish her new clipping mat for Christmas and this would be laid down in front of the fire-place. Everything was clean and smart and my mam would have made a Christmas cake with almond icing and some bottles of green ginger wine. This was the strongest drink I could ever imagine, as it would make my throat burn. It gave me the hiccups or 'essics' as I called them. My wine was well watered down to solve the problem.

My dad's favourite cake was spiced loaf and our Christmas cake was a rich version of this. It had a short life and a merry one, as my mam would give callers such generous slices with their wine.

In the months leading up to Christmas, she would order packets of cigarettes, with her groceries from the store. These would be stacked up in the bottom of the sideboard,

Durham wives took a pride in their shining range

Woodbines, Players and Capstan. In the week prior to Christmas, these were handed out to the club men, the grocer, the baker, the butcher and the milkman. All the regular callers were offered cake and ginger wine, wished a Merry Christmas and given their present. Most were smokers and very appreciative. We always had a newspaper delivered, The Daily Herald. The paper boy was not to be outdone and would knock on the door with the paper on Christmas Eve. My mam would answer the door. "Bah, you know this is the only time you can't get the paper through the letter box," she thought aloud. "There you are pet, Merry Christmas," as she gave him a shilling. "Oh! – thank you," the lad would look surprised, "and the same to you missus", as he grinned and whisked away with his heavy bag.

When it was bedtime, my dad would put an enormous log on the fire so that Santa could step on this when he came down the chimney, so he wouldn't burn his feet. Marvelling at the thought of Santa coming down our chimney with his big sack of toys, I would lie in bed and try to puzzle out, how he could get around all those houses in one night, the roofs, the chimney pots, all to negotiate, and never a slip to be made. What a marvellous man he must be, looking after and coping with so many children. I wasn't silly, I knew that Santa didn't fly over roof tops, but he did come in the snow with his sledge, drawn by reindeer. Though it must have been hard going when we had no snow, which sometimes happened. Experience had taught me that it was not easy to pull a sledge without snow. I had a sneaking feeling that he didn't come down all those chimneys, but through the doors of some homes.

Nevertheless at the age of four, I was a firm believer in Santa Claus, I had seen him, and what is more revered him and feared him, as I did Doctor Wardle and God, in that order. A glass of wine and a large slice of Christmas cake was always left on the kitchen table for him. Sure enough in the morning the cake had gone, the wine glass was empty and there were bulging stockings and presents on the mat. Emptying the stockings was always a great thrill. I once had a whistle and a penknife, with some candy rock. And always, an orange and an apple. I got a bazooka, and another time, a mouth organ, that my dad taught me how to play. There was such excitement, my mam would get a box of chocolates, some nuts and an orange. To our great surprise and delight, my dad would have just a potato, some walnuts and a whole lot of cinders that Santa put there just for fun. We all had a good laugh at my dad at his surprise and remarks when he emptied his stocking. I will never forget what great fun and excitement we had, with such simple objects. Thinking back, I feel so sorry for children of the affluent society, who never experience such joy and fun.

Oh what a thrill, when I had a pop-gun from Santa. This must have been the world's most un-lethal weapon. Even the cork that it fired was on a piece of string, but it was effective against a row of cardboard soldiers at close range. I would lie on the clipping mat in front of the fire and shoot them down. Another time I had a tin pea shooter in my Christmas stocking. Hard dry peas were the best ammunition, but sometimes I had to make do with pearl barley – oh yes, times were hard in those days. Later I had a wooden tommy gun for my birthday of which I was very proud. There was a spring and ratchet that made a loud rat-tat-tat sound as you turned the handle. Very realistic, just like on the pictures.

One Christmas I shall never forget was when my dad had made a swing with rope and a wooden seat. This was fixed from large eye bolts through the pantry door frame. The door was wedged open, and I could swing to my heart's content.

His method of drilling holes through the door frame on that occasion, was to drill small holes first with a gimlet, which was like a corkscrew, with a wooden handle used for boring holes. The great thrill to me was the next stage, which was the enlargement of the holes to take the big eye-bolts. First of all, he would stoke the fire up well, to get it nice and red. Then in would go the poker, to the middle of the glowing coals. After a a few minutes, he would pull out the poker and say, "Ar think that's hot enough, cherry red". Then, to the pantry door frame. In went the glowing poker to the first small hole. Oh what a hiss and clouds of white smoke. The smell was like no other smell, burning paint and wood, which soon enveloped the kitchen and rest of the house. Mam exclaimed, "Bah Fred, what are you doin', makin' such a styth, you should open the windows?" "Come out of the way" he replied, as he lunged the poker back into the fire to heat it again. Then,"Mind out, this is hot", as he hurried to the waiting holes, in case the poker cooled off before he got there. At last, after several attacks, the holes were big enough, although black and charred.

In went the eyebolts, with washers and nuts. The swing was ready to test and my dad lifted me on the seat and began to gently push me, as I swung to and fro. This was better than the swings in the rec, as I swung between kitchen and pantry. "But how am Ar goin' to get in and out of the pantry" wondered my mam, aloud. My dad produced a large nail, which he soon hammered into the door frame at the side. "There you are, just pull the swing like this", as he hooked it over the nail. "Bah, you have a clever dad" she said. I thought he was the cleverest dad in the world.

Christmas dinners were of little importance in my young years, the only meat that we ever had was beef or mutton from our butcher. Goose, chicken and pork, were talked about only, with great suspicion and never contemplated as meat for our table, not even at Christmas. For afters, we always had Christmas cake, never the traditional pudding. Rum sauce was never used, as being Methodists, there was no alcohol in our house.

The Christmas cake was always gone by New Year's Eve, when my mam would produce her New Year's cake, out of a tin where she had been keeping it. This was a replica of the Christmas cake and received the same treatment until it was all devoured.

There were the folks out the back, with which we had closer contact, than with the folks out the front. Our back street was cobbled with hard blue brick paviors, not just muck like many around. This was not a pitty area, although on the edge of the Durham coalfield. The cobbles were clean and blue and ran all the way down the back street to the road, Grey Street. Wives always used to empty their boiling potato or pea water between the cobbles to kill the weeds which grew there. In the top house was Mr and Mrs Hughes. He was a maintenance fitter at the local dairy as it was known, the store milk processing and bottling plant, next to the bakery.

The dairy was the noisiest place I could imagine, with the loud clanging of the empty churns and the rattle of bottles in crates. Over all this, was the background hum of machinery and the hiss of steam. The dairy women added to the din, with their coarse and vulgar shouting. These turbanned dairy maids, with their red rubber aprons and turned-down black wellies were far removed from their nursery rhyme image. Oh!, if milk bottles could talk, they could tell some tales!

I expect Mr Hughes was pleased when he was heading home from work, up our back street. He always wore spectacles and a cloth cap, with his blue boiler suit always open, – no buttons. It must have been the heat. When he spied me on our back step, he would usually shout, "Come here, Ar'll cut your head off and put a cabbage on". I would run into the yard, then come back and peep, for I knew by his kindly face, that it was only fun. His wife was plump, with a pleasant rosy complexion. I thought she was "Mrs USE" because of the way that Mrs Pallister dropped her aitches. The Pallisters were second door down across our back street.

Mr Pallister worked at the store, as a lorry driver and Mrs Pallister was a good friend of my mam. They were always gossiping in the back street. Their daughter Eileen was my first sweetheart and about my age, a little blonde bombshell, who I am sure was spoiled by Percy and Peggy Pallister, as they had lost their first child, Sheila, as a baby. Theirs was an open house and more kind and generous people you would never meet in the whole of County Durham. This was my second home and I spent many hours there as a youngster, playing games in worlds of make believe under the table or under the stairs.

They doted on Eileen, as one could understand, she was their pride and joy. A photographer would sometimes come around knocking on doors to take your picture. Mrs Pallister thought that was a nice idea and quickly spruced us up, as the man set up his wooden legged tripod and camera on the pavement. "Watch the dickie bird". Click, and one of my most treasured photo's was created. Anyone could walk through their house, from front to back and take whatever they liked, Mrs Pallister would be across the back lane engrossed in deep conversation with my mam or some other neighbour. The subject was not world politics, current affairs, the rise of Hitler or any other such piffle, but the cost of sugar, rationing, children's shoes, coupons, gas masks etc. Bishop housewives always wore aprons or pinnies before the war, at least they did in our street. The pinnies were worn for housework, cooking, making jam, making mats. Whatever the task, the pinnie was appropriate. They gossiped on their back steps, wearing pinnies. For going to the shops the pinnies came off and hung on the pantry door. They were exchanged for a coat and hat. My mam had a turban which was very fashionable then, with her hair made up into a kind of roll. I don't know how she kept it like that, always so neat and tidy.

Eileen was very spoiled as I have already said. She would interrupt her mother continually during conversation. Her mam was unperturbed and just carried on regardless. I will always remember Eileen getting hold of her mother's hands and climbing up her, walking fashion, up her legs, onto her pinnie and so upward. When her shoes reached her mam's neck, she would swing over backwards in a somersault hands still clasped until she landed safely back on the ground. This was during a deep conversation with my mam as they chatted away in the back street.

Snow White and The Seven Dwarfs was at the Odeon and my mam took me to see it. I thought this was a magical experience and collected the pottery figures of the dwarfs, from Woolworths and knew all their names. They gradually got broken and thrown out over the years. Eileen had a big cardboard cut-out figure of Shirley Temple, who was a favourite at the pictures. The figure was complete with different kinds of cardboard dresses, which she could wear for different occasions. What great fun she had with her screen idol.

My dad took me to the Odeon to see Erol Flynn, in 'Robin Hood'. This was the most exciting film I had ever seen. I still think it beats all the other versions which have been made since then. Erol Flynn as Robin Hood, is pure

The man with the tripod came – 'Watch the dickie bird'

nostalgia to me! What bravado! – dumping the royal deer on the table in front of Prince John.

New snowfall made the world look like fairyland, that sparkled in the sunshine. My eyes would squint as I made my way to the rec, with squeaking wellies, plodding towards the swings. For winter, our dads made us sledges with iron runners and a rope to pull with. Toboggan was a word we never heard, sledges were all the rage in 1940 when I was five.

One fateful day, that January, before my baby sister was born, I had been out in the snow, sledging with my friends in the morning and must have been feeling very tired, when there was a knock at the back door after dinner. My mam shouted, "Brian, it's Dorothy asking if you are goin' out sledgin' again?" I replied, "No, Ar'm stayin' in". It was good to feel warm again, I wanted to play inside by the fire with my lead aeroplanes and soldiers.

I knew nothing of what happened that dreadful day, until I heard later from my mam and dad. Nobody told me anything, as though I would not understand. Dorothy, after failing to raise me, went over to the Pallisters to see if Eileen was coming out to sledge. Eileen's mam soon had her suitably wellied, mufflered and mittened, with a nice warm coat over her tartan kilt. They were having great fun as you can imagine, the ice was great and the sledge run was very fast. Eileen's sledge ran out of the end of her little street onto Grey Street, the main road. She collided with a coal delivery lorry.

What a catastrophe. Somebody ran for the doctor, the ambulance, but to no avail. Eileen was dead. Mrs Pallister heard news of the accident as she chatted by the back gate and couldn't think of it being Eileen, "She's only sledgin' in our front street". Until they said, the little girl was wearing a tartan kilt. I don't know how Mr and Mrs Pallister coped with that devastating news of their beloved Eileen. They must have had great resilience to come out of that tragedy. What a cruel and sudden loss. I didn't understand at all about death and was only told that Eileen had, "Gone to Jesus, to be an angel". My mam couldn't console Mrs Pallister, who laid thrashing on the floor, screaming in grief. I remember seeing Eileen's grave in Bishop cemetery with an angel headstone. I shed tears to this day when I hear the hymn, that we often sang in Sunday School.

> *There's a Friend for little children*
> *Above the bright blue sky,*
> *A Friend who never changeth,*
> *Whose love can never die.*
> *Unlike our friends by nature,*
> *Who change with changing years,*
> *This Friend is always worthy*
> *The precious Name he bears.*

I felt in my heart of hearts, that she was in safe hands. The finger of time moved on. Only time could begin to heal such a wound. The Pallisters were later to be blessed with a beautiful baby boy, 'Our John.'

One day my mam said to me, "If you collect lots of silver paper you can have a baby brother or sister". This was no doubt to prepare me for the intrusion that they intended. It was always my mam that was pushing for a baby, as if our little Brian, wasn't enough.

My sister was born in 'The Home,' that is, in the nursing home in Princes Street, that was the birth place of many before and since. The big Weetabix box in the bedroom had finally paid off and was cashed in for a bairn. "How did you choose from all those cots, with babies". "Oh, we just picked a nice little sister for you – why do you ask questions?" My Dad had no part in the matter, he was always at work, stooping in holes in the road and smiling up at people.

Our new baby was christened Elizabeth, but always called Bette. "BETTE" my mam would spell out to people, "Yer know, like Bette Davis", who was all the rage at the pictures. At least it was more imaginative than Brian. My name was to have been Stanley, but there was a change at the last minute. On reflection I am not a Stan, Laurel or otherwise, but a Brian, strong like a lion. I was so pleased and proud to have a little sister and thought that they had made a good choice from all those cots with babies in them. Sometimes whilst lying in bed before sleep, I would try to imagine what it would be like if my mam and dad had brought some other baby, instead of Bette. I would panic at the thought of Bette in someone else's house, then feel a great relief when I heard that unmistakeable crying from the next room.

CHAPTER 5

ADVENTURES

On the periphery of my young world, there was a shop in Grey Street, run by Walter Paley and his wife Edna. He was adept at wrapping small quantities of sweets in squares of paper, folded into a cornet shape. He had bulls eyes, aniseed balls, spanish and sherbet and other exotic sweets, which were in abundance before the war. My favourite was sherbet, a kind of fizzy powder in a paper tube, that tingled on your tongue when you sucked it out through a black liquorice straw. Afterwards you ate the straw –delicious. Paleys sold anything you could ever want for your day to day living and my mam would often send me down there with a little basket and a note for groceries or something for dad's tea.

Further down the back street were the Parkers, who had Sheila, older than me and Bobby, a bit younger. Eileen, Bobby and me had been playmates and spent our early years in the back street, playing with our marbles and catching bumble bees in jam jars. Little Bobby who was much smaller than myself, would come to call for me, clutching his jam jar. "Is Brian coming out to catch bumblers?" followed by two raspberries – this was a strange little habit of his. Off we would go up to the rec, for great adventures in the jungles of long grass and wild flowers.

You got a jam jar, put some holes in the lid for breathing, then you went bumbling by catching a bumble bee, often with a dandelion head.

Soon we became skilled hunters. We had to be careful and quick, to avoid getting stung. Before long we would return home with our buzzing jars of bumblers, complete with clover and dandelion heads. "Bah, that's clever" my mam would admire. Then "Ar think their mammies 'll wonder where they are. Now you'd better let them go, back through the rec railings." And I would do that, by lying the jar in the grass through the railings, before removing the lid. Off they would fly, to be home just in time for tea.

My first educational magazine was the Beano, which I got every week. I looked forward with anticipation to the continuing adventures of the characters. There was Big Eggo the ostrich, Lord Snooty and his pals, Desperate Dan, with his cow pie, Pansy Potter, the strong man's daughter. This comic must have had American origins as some of the words were foreign to me. They would be eating big slices of melon or pomegranates, unknown to us. When the war was over, I would have lots of melons and pomegranates, as well as bananas. My mouth would water in anticipation. As for hurricanes and tornados these were complete mysteries to me.

There were some things in my young life that struck terror into me. My mam had a Be-Ro cookery book, with recipes. This was a long thin book with a picture of a woman baking, on the front cover. However I looked at this woman, she had a wolf's face, which terrifed me, evil looking like the wolf in Red Riding Hood. Even though I was frightened, I would still take a peep at this wolf woman. I think the vee neck of her dress looked like an extension of her chin.

There was a Golden Book of Wonder, that I had one birthday. This was full of interesting things, lots of pictures and stories. One of those stories was about, Nose The Dwarf, an ugly little man. The character that really frightened me was the Wicked Witch. Although I loved that book I dreaded the page showing the witch holding a severed head by its long hair, over a cauldron and wished I could have torn this out and burned it. One creature that filled me with dread and horror was the spider. Even now I have great revulsion if I have to remove a spider from the bath, a newspaper or magazine is an essential tool. When I was very small, my mam would always bake her own bread and I would help her to knead the dough on the kitchen table. She would usually send me to Paley's shop for two penn'orth of yeast.

They always had fresh yeast for baking. The dough would be divided into portions and placed into the baking tins, covered with a damp tea-towel, to rise on the hearth. I loved to nibble at the yeast and my mam would usually have some left over. "There you are Brian, you can finish off this yeast", she always pronounced it 'yest'.

She also would make what she called, new bread, I think the recipe was different to ordinary bread. This dough would be rolled out into a flat sheet, then cut into squares and placed on a flat tray to rise before going into the oven. This was best eaten warm from the oven, with butter and jam. When a loaf of bread was sliced, there were often little hollow cavities with fine webs where the dough had expanded. In my own mind, I imagined that these webs had been made by spiders and despite reassurance to the contrary, would cut out those bits to be left on the side of my plate. When we were going to the seaside, my gram-ma would make 'ned cakes', which were flat and square, very heavy, not like my mam's new bread. These were good fillers for hungry bairns, but no good for swimming, you might sink.

We had evacuees from coastal towns, that were likely to be bombed when war was imminent. My folks must have volunteered to take them, but I knew nothing of this of course, until Walter appeared. His sister Ruth went to the Pallisters' house. Walter was older than me, he went to school before I started and I don't remember much about him now, except that he was a big boy, probably eight or nine. My mam remarked, "That boy doesn't say much, but he watches every bite Ar eat at mealtimes". He had his ration book, which my mam took charge of, as he was in her care. Walter was from Gateshead-on-Tyne. My mam said his dad was a butcher, but he sent us no meat. Parcels came for Walter and he would disappear upstairs to his bedroom – that is, my bedroom – to open them. The only evidence of what was in his parcels, were the sweet papers left on the lavatory floor. The one and only toilet in our home, was across the yard next to the coal house. Very posh it was, a water closet, but always called, the lav. There were only two ways to describe how you visited the toilet. "Just going to the lav", or ladies and sisters would say, "Just popping across the yard", as though to feed the birds. Walter went to the lav to indulge in his parcel, but hadn't the savvy to flush away the evidence. Poor Walter, these are my only memories of him.

In the rec, there were sandpits, swings, rings, a teapot lid, a slide and an ocean wave. Also there was a bandstand with names embellished on shields around the railings; Beethoven, Mozart, Brahms, etc. I recall a band, but not what they played. There was a putting green, bowls and tennis. My dad didn't play bowls or tennis, however he did play the harmonica. "Oh get your mouth organ out dad," we would plead and he would entertain us with music, especially if we had visitors. We would sing or accompany him, with paper and comb. This must have been a dreadful sound by any musical standard, but sweet to our ears. A cup was a great asset as an amplifier, as mutes are used with trumpets, to give some expression. He would play well known Geordie songs that everybody knew and could join in singing, like, Keep Your Feet Still Geordie Hinnie, Cushie Butterfield, Blaydon Races, Bobby Shafto's Gone to Sea, The Keel Row, or wartime favourites, popularised on the wireless; Run Rabbit Run, When the Fuhrer Says, Who Do You Think You Are Kidding Mr Hitler, There'll Be Blue Birds Over. These were great morale boosters for the British people. We never realised how near we were to being invaded and overrun by the enemy, just as well.

My dad made a hoop and hook for me to play with. These were hung in the coalhouse until the season. In the spring everyone got their hoops, skipping ropes or tops and whips out. The hoops were iron rings about three feet in diameter. You could bool them with your hook and guide them where you wanted. Some boys had tyres, from rubbish tips which they booled by hand.

Near to us, there was a bakery, dairy and a slaughter

house, all part of the store buildings. The bakery produced lovely smells of fresh baked bread, pies and cakes. The dairy pasteurised and bottled milk, collected from farms early each morning. Mr Pallister was a lorry driver and one of the early morning collectors from the far flung farms. The milk was pasteurised and suitably watered to make up the spillages and pilferages. Water did no-one any harm, so why worry?

Ah! but the most thrilling and disturbing aspect was the slaughter house. This is where sheep, cows and pigs were turned into meat!. Now as young lads playing around outside the slaughter house, we used to see the process being carried out through a grating in the wall. The beast were brought on the hoof in those days, easier and cheaper than cattle trucks, at least on short journeys. They were driven through the streets from the cattle mart to their destination and hence to your dinner table just like The Overlanders, a film of that era, but in real life. I recall the thrill of seeing those beast being herded past the end of our back street, to their final field. This was not a green field, but muddy and deep in cow muck. A sad field. The unhappy beast were then taken to the hunger house, where they mooed loud and long, awaiting execution. I think pigs and sheep were brought in lorries and not herded through the streets. There was a cattle herder, a little hunchback, clad in a dirty brown, stained smock. He brandished a big stick. That stick made him a big man, like a Nazi with a gun. This little man was to be found at the cattle market, poking and prodding the beast with his stick and whacking them to make them move. Perhaps he got satisfaction out of whacking cows, instead of women, whom he would love to whack because they rejected him as an outcast.

As bairns, we always looked out for the thrill of the cattle drive, which was once a week, the day of the livestock market or 'mart' as it was known. Despite the drovers and a couple of skilful dogs, there was the odd beast that was determined not to complete the one way trip. Once there was a beast which went mad, beserk and broke away from the herd, charging up our back lane. Dogs and washing flew in all directions and the wives gathered up their young and disappeared behind the hastily locked gates of their safe back yards. Cats loping on the high brick walls and coal house roofs, looked on in dismay. The frantic beast bolted round the end of the back street and disappeared into the distance followed by the cursing hunchback and his dogs.

As a girl in Newbottle, my mam had been frightened by a cow that poked its head over their half door, bellowing. The imprint on her mind was never forgotten. If cattle came into sight, she would just go into the nearest door that would open, no matter whose house or shop, in complete terror until it was safe to emerge.

Beyond the slaughter house, were the stables where all the cart horses were kept. There was a resident horsekeeper, Mr Bell whose house formed a link between the slaughter house and the stable block. There were many horses, as they were the main means of delivery transport for the butcher, the baker and the grocer. We had several horse drawn deliveries each week.

Of these I shall never forget a man called Harry Wright, a cheery man, who wore a light brown smock and a cloth cap. He came to deliver our grocery order. The order man came regularly, once a week to write down your order. This

The Store stables and slaughter house

was duly made up and delivered, wrapped in brown paper and string in the following week. It worked like clockwork and you got dividend on what you spent. You always quoted your membership number, which went onto your bill. Armies of girl clerks processed the bills, so that dividend could be allocated against your number. When the dividend was declared, my mam immediately set about spending the money on things she couldn't normally afford and certainly didn't need.

Harry Wright's cart was very large, with four great wooden spoked wheels, with iron tyres, that rumbled and crunched the stones as it came laden up our street. There was a great, green canvas canopy over a framework that covered the cart. Inside were racks of parcels, orders neatly wrapped and tied with string, each with a name and number. His horse was Toby, a magnificent, strong and obedient animal. He would pull all day or stand all day, whatever his master wished. One day, Harry let me climb up into the seat next to him. What a wonderful experience for a small boy, the hard wooden bench seat, the big brake handle that clamped the wooden brake blocks onto the wheels. In addition to this, there was an iron footrail and bar over which the leather reins came into the driver's weather beaten strong hands. The swishing tail, the huge hindquarters of Toby, the shafts, harness and blinkers. The smell of horse and horsemuck was like magic. There were oil lamps on each side for when it got dark.

After that first encounter, I couldn't settle until I got my mam to ask if I could have a ride with Harry on his cart. That was my ambition, to drive a cart like this, with Toby. It was a winter's afternoon when my mam wrapped me up in a scarf and knitted mitts before lifting me in place next to Harry, my Wild West Wagon Train Hero. I know it was winter because Toby was snorting 'steam' from his nostrils and Harry was breathing a ghostly breath. "Bah! Mrs Joslin, too cold for snow", he said. Then, "Are you ready bonnie lad?" I hung onto the back of my seat and nervously nodded. At this, Harry reached for the big brake handle and pushed it forward, at the same time saying, "Gid up boy" and he flipped the reins that ran through brass rings on Toby's collar and then fixed to his mouth in some way I couldn't fathom out at the time. The great backside started moving from side to side and we started moving down the street. What a thrill, my mam waving. "Be a good boy now," and we were off.

This was my first experience of locomotion from such a high viewpoint, from where I could look down on the world around. "All right pet" and he gave me a sweet. We took the bend at high speed into Grey Street and away towards 'Indian Territory'. What a thrill, the clip clop of the hooves, the crunch of the wheels on the hard road, the snorting, the swish of the tail. Words cannot describe how I felt at the age of five, to have this wonderful experience, the cold wind in my ears, the flapping of the canvas sheeting, the smell of horse and hay and paraffin was a new experience, the elixir of life. This ride had definitely settled my career when I grew up. As Harry stopped to deliver his parcels, he let me hold the reins. The kindly Bishop folk would say, "Bah, aren't you a lucky boy to get a ride up there" or "Hello pet, eeh, it's Brian, Ar'll tell yer mam Ar've seen yer". This made me feel so proud.

It turned dark soon and Harry lit the lamps and they flickered as we continued on our round. All the parcels were duly delivered and Toby was pleased to trot home to the stables for supper in his warm stall. We joined other carts as we passed under the arch into the stable yard. Harry helped me down and I watched him unhitch Toby and remove his harness and trappings, which he hung on the wall inside the stables. Toby was lead, clip-clopping over the cobbles into his stall next to his mates, who were already champing away at their meal of 'choppy', crushed oats and hay. Harry took me round home, which wasn't far and my dad was already back from work, it was about six o'clock and dark.

My mam and dad were pleased that I had enjoyed my adventure and said, "Bah, your cheeks are rosy" it must have worked wonders for my sallow complexion. I had some chips and beans, my favourite meal, with buttered bread and a pot of sweet tea. I slept like a log as you can imagine, dreaming of my great adventure. Not long afterwards I got a long winter coat at Doggarts which I called my Harry Wright coat, my favourite. Further trips on Harry's cart never repeated that first enchanted journey around the streets of Bishop, on that frosty winter's day.

CHAPTER 6

GROWING PAINS

Besides the regular visits of the club man from the store and Doggarts, there was the Doctors Woman, who would come once a fortnight. Her face was heavily made up, with bright pink cheeks, which my mam said was rouge. She was tall and slim, with a black coat and hat, a sombre woman. She would have been more suited as an undertaker's woman, with her get-up. This fund was essential to working class families before the National Health Service, in case of illness and hospital treatment, which all had to be paid for. As well as the Doctor's Club, my mam and dad paid into the Forresters and the Rechabites, both friendly societies, tuppence a week as I recall to insure against illness or hard times.

We always seemed to have long hot summers in the early war years, when we would spend many long hours playing in the cosy back street or chalking on the front pavement. Toy tanks and aeroplanes were all the rage. My dad once made me some lead aeroplanes for Christmas. I'll never forget the tacky brown paint that came off on my fingers, as I zoomed about in the back street or in the kitchen, making aeroplane noises, dive bombing and machine gunning. These battles were far more real to me than the modern day TV games. But how could I think that then, television was a thing of the future, as far as I was concerned.

We did have a wireless though, which was an Ekco, the twin of Pallisters. I later learned that these sets were obtained by Mr Pallister from the store, no doubt at a discounted price. It was the first wireless that we possessed and took pride of place on a shelf my dad had made from an electric meter board, high up on the kitchen wall. This wireless set seemed very large to me and had a brown bakelite case, the first plastic which had been developed, that could be moulded into shape. It had a gold coloured cloth panel on the front, where the sound came from. How the sound got there, I couldn't imagine, it was like a magic box. There was a long glass dial which lit up when you switched on, with a pointer that travelled to places around the World when you turned a knob. Daventry, Droitwich, Hilversum, Berlin, were names I recall, on that magical dial. This wireless must have held a great fascination for me, I could only reach it by climbing upon the back of our couch. It drew me like a magnet and inevitably I managed to bring it off the shelf whilst twiddling the knobs. There was an enormous crash and my mam was vexed as there was a large chunk of bakelite broken out of one corner, which was to remain like that for ever. The snapped flex and aerial were left dangling. I'm still a compulsive knob twiddler, never learned my lesson!

When my dad came in from work, he parked his bike in the yard as usual and I dreaded the worst. He was not angry, but I think relieved. "So long as the bairn's alright" he said, as he stroked my head. When he'd finished his tea, he took the back off the set and had a good look. "The valves seem intact" he pronounced. He soon had it back on the shelf and connected up. It always took about five minutes for the valves to warm up before the sound came out. The dial lit up and we waited. That was a long five minutes, but the music was the sweeter when it came playing through, to everyone's relief. They don't make them like that any more. This, as you can imagine provided a new topic of conversation for my mam and Mrs Pallister. If this had been broken, I doubt whether we could have found anyone to repair it. It would have had to be sent away, which meant it could take between two weeks and forever, to come back.

At least our set didn't suffer the fate of Geordie Chapman's wireless. Now Geordie was a workmate of my dad's, a canny lad my dad thought, lived in Shildon. One night, Geordie was on his hunkers in front of the fire with the mat rolled back. He was chopping sticks on the stone flags, which was a common practice then and left no mess. You didn't even have to sweep it under the carpet, just put the mat back. Geordie was happily chopping away, listening to the wireless. There was a crackle and a whistle, the programme was interrupted by a German station. This was William Joyce, an English collaborator and traitor, working for the Nazis, pouring out propaganda to demoralise the British people with his lies. He was better known as Lord Hawhaw and hated, for what he was. Geordie became so incensed by this traitor that he sprang at the wireless like a Viking warrior and buried his axe into it. The sound of breaking glass and bakelite put an immediate end to Lord Hawhaw's tauntings. "That'll learn that bastard to come shoutin in here," he spat with great satisfaction. That programme was axed, you might say!

Gas masks were issued to everyone and we had to go to St Peter's Church Hall in Stranton Street to be fitted out with the right size and be shown how to put them on and breathe through them. The smell of rubber hit you as you went through the door. My dad already had his gas mask, which had an elephant's trunk, and also a tin hat, for fire watching, so that only mam, Bette and me, had to be kitted out. Bette was in her pram, as she was only a few months old. Some younger boys and girls had Micky Mouse gas masks, with red ears I think, I suppose to make it easier for mothers to get them to put them on. "Howay pet, get yer Micky Mouse mask on," they would say encouragingly. Mine was a proper gas mask with white straps and buckles and a shiny filter. There was a celluloid panel to look out of which soon got steamed up. The tight black rubber had a strong new smell and made a suggestive noise when you breathed out, which caused great mirth and merriment. My mam's mask was like mine, but a bigger size.

Now Bette had to lie inside a khaki coloured respirator,

which was then closed up. Mam had to pump it like a concertina so that she could breathe. You can imagine that my little sister didn't care for this idea and bawled the place down. I think she would rather be gassed than be suffocated in that machine of torture, but how could babies understand the evils of war? All kitted out, we had to write our names on our gas mask boxes. I proudly walked home with my mam, holding onto the pram, with my new cardboard gas mask box slung around my neck by its cord.

I recall during a hot summer's day, sitting on the kerb with Bobby Parker at the bottom of our street, bursting large bubbles that appeared in the tar at the road edge. It must have been very hot to bubble like that. It was only after being engrossed in this interesting and fascinating pastime for some while, poking with matchsticks and fingers, that we realised that tar was sticky stuff. Even when you tried to wipe it off on your trousers it wouldn't shift, but it did mess up everything you touched. There was no way out, we had to go home to face the music. My mam

Trying on gas masks

was not pleased, you might say. She was vexed at the sight of me and my clothes and gave my legs a good smacking. I remember sitting on the kitchen table, my legs smarting and crying with tears running down my cheeks whilst she spent ages rubbing butter into the tar on my hands and arms to clean off the mess. I was sent to bed and sobbed bitterly. On reflection, I think this was harsh treatment for a little boy who was just exploring and experimenting with the natural world, not being naughty.

My dad came in from work, he had a very soft heart. He came to my bed and said, "Don't worry pet, Ar forgive you" and gave me a hug. He realised that my mam had been harsh on me.

His words worked wonders and made me feel better. He told me a story about the house with the windows of gold, and we said our prayers together, before I fell into a deep sleep of relief. If I'd been really naughty, then I would have taken my punishment readily, as I did many times during my school years. Injustice hurt me then, as it does now. Woe betide anyone who treats me unjustly. This philosophy has won me battles in life, that seemed impossible to win at the outset. The pursuit of justice is a tremendous driving force – but I am rambling on with thoughts I could not comprehend at the time. I hope I have always learned lessons from my many mistakes in life.

They built a large circular tank, like a swimming pool in the middle of the road at the bottom of our street. This was filled with water for fire fighting, in case of incendiary bomb attacks. I could just look over the rim to see the great expanse of water. These steel tanks were constructed in other streets around the town, in preparation for what might happen in war. They became great places to play around, the big boys would sail pieces of wood, which were ships and bomb them with stones, only to be chased away by irate neighbours, when the action got too noisy. The water soon became green and smelly but still alright for putting out fires.

We were encouraged to go out into the woods and hedgerows to collect as many red rose hips as we could, in our spare time. We were quite used to going brambling, so we often would kill two birds with one stone. An enamelled milk can, was used for brambles and a paper bag for rose hips. The hips were weighed at school and we were paid fourpence a pound. These were to be made into rose hip syrup, which is rich in Vitamin C.

There was also a continual drive during the war to recycle paper and jars, especially jam jars. Bread and jam were part of the staple diet of working class families and it was easy to collect large quantities, by going around knocking on doors. People were asked to save their jam jars and these were always washed and clean. When we had collected a full barrow load, these were taken to the store. When they had been checked and counted, you were paid a farthing each. You could soon earn yourself a few shillings. A tanner for two dozen jars, money for old rope. Another thing we did was to collect old beer bottles from dustbins. We would then hawk these around all the public houses and could collect the ha'penny or penny deposit. Us lads got to know all the public houses, especially in Bondgate, where they were in abundance. I recall the Bay Horse, The Wheatsheaf, and The Sun Inn, which was later painstakingly dismantled, and rebuilt at the famous Beamish Museum. Those that nobody claimed, were used for catapult practice, lined up on a fence or water tower wall.

In those days little girls of nine or ten, would offer to take your baby out for a walk, in its pram. This was often done and no harm in it, not so many perverts about, but some, nevertheless. Patsy, was about nine years old, and lived down our back way, below Pallisters. She came to our house one day to ask if she could take the baby out into the rec. My mam was probably ready for a rest and so agreed. She soon got Bette ready, sat her in the pram, and off Patsy went, into the rec, on that glorious sunny afternoon. She had been gone about half an hour or so, when the air-raid sirens sounded. "Eeh it's the sirens", cried my mam. Panicking, she made a beeline for the rec. She passed Patsy, running home in haste, minus the pram. This was neatly parked with its brake on, next to the bench where Patsy had been sitting. Bette was sat there quite happily sucking a Rusk. Fortunately the Luftwaffe weren't bombing that day and the all clear was soon sounded. This brought an abrupt end to such outings.

Collecting waste paper for the War Effort

My mam used to knit in her spare time and also made clipping mats, especially in the winter evenings. "Ar've got some good clippin's" she would say to Mrs Pallister "Ar think Ar'll have a mat in the frames, d'yer think Mr Pallister could get me a sugar bag". They always used formal titles, never first names, although they were good friends. My mam was always Mrs Jozlen – so pronounced by Mrs Pallister. Clippings, were strips of cloth, usually wool, that were cut from old clothes and came in whatever colours happened to be available at the time. Everybody in Durham working class homes, especially in coalmining areas, had a set of wooden mat frames, where a base of sackcloth was stitched in and stretched to form the base of the mat. With progger and clippings, you could make it whatever shape and pattern you liked.

On one occasion, Bette was sat in the cardboard box with the clippings, to keep her amused whilst my mam laboured on the mat frame. This usually spanned between the edge of the table and a chair back, so that you could get to both sides of the mat. We had lino on the floor, which had a pattern like wood blocks and was very shiny and slippery. I soon discovered that I could run and slide on this, in my stocking feet, only to fall on my backside and slide further. This activity thrilled our Bette, who had never seen the likes before and she shrieked with laughter. Each time I fell, her eyes would close with laughter as they do to this day. This is a vivid memory. "Now stop it Brian" my mam said, "she'll go into a kink." I never knew what a kink was, but have just looked it up in a medical encyclopedia – a kind of fit. I'm glad I stopped, it could have ruined her life! Who would want a kinky sister?

Looking down our small street from the front door you could see trains passing, as the line was near. The station was not far away and I would often go there with my pals,

Bette in her new bonnet, with a friend

to see the trains from the railway bridge, near the cattle field. There was a big water tank near the track side, not far from the bottom of our street, opposite the bakery. This is where the engines came to be filled with water and we used to sit on the high stone wall that bounded the railway line, to watch this fascinating operation.

The train driver would always wave to us, as he drove the great engine slowly into place by the side of the water tank. The fireman would climb up on top of the engine and open a lid to take the water. There was a big pipe from the water tank, which was swung into place and a leather hose like an elephant's trunk which he pushed into the engine.

Once all was in place, he pulled a rope that was hanging down from a valve. There was a loud gurgling noise as the elephant's trunk filled with water and wriggled as this went splashing down into the engine. It was a big pipe and not long before the water was brimming out of the tank and running down each side onto the cinder track. He pulled another rope and the water stopped. The big pipe was pushed away on its swinging arm, dripping water.

Having drunk its fill, the engine rested, breathing slowly and deeply, like a dragon. There were lots of polished copper pipes and brass gauges that shone brightly in the orange light, when the fireman opened the fire door with his shovel. With a clang and swish, shovels of coal were shot through the open door onto the waiting fire, from the gleaming black pile behind. The beast breathed out wisps of grey smoke from its massive black funnel, which made our eyes blink when it drifted towards us. Pure white steam gently hissed from the cylinders down by the wheels, whilst oil and water dripped onto the shining iron rails and cinders beneath.

The engine driver would reach up to blow his whistle and his dirty face would burst into laughter, as we boys started with suprise and nearly fell off the wall. There were a series of slow, long puffs like blowing dandelion heads. One o'clock – two o'clock – three o'clock. The mighty pistons squirted steam and shining rods pushed the massive wheels into motion. The engine trundled along to the station, rested and refreshed, ready to pull its train of coals to Newcastle or passengers to far flung parts of the

Just Resting

Empire. There was never any thought of danger by ourselves or parents in our sitting on high walls overlooking the railway or whether we ventured onto the track, which we did. We used to put ha'pennies on the line to make them into pennies, as they squashed out flat by a passing train. Sometimes we tried to pass these off for a penn'orth of sweets at Paley's shop. It never worked, but was good fun.

CHAPTER 7

GOING THROUGH HOME

The train fare from Bishop to Fencehouses must have been cheap. My mam would often take Bette and me to her mother's for the day. "Ar think we'll go through home for the day Fred", she would remark. My grandmother was known as, gram-ma, always without the 'd'. She lived at Houghton-le-Spring, near to Newbottle, the village of my birth. This was the Sunderland train which passed through Durham City and on to Fencehouses, where we got off. From there we would walk across a field to the main road which took us to gram-ma's house at Homelands, a council estate on the edge of Houghton. It took about half an hour to walk there from the station. Sometimes my dad would be with us but not often, he was either at work, out preaching or at some meeting to do with the chapel.

Gram-ma's was very posh to me as a small boy. I'd never seen such luxury, with a bathroom and toilet. It was a special treat to get bathed there, where hot and cold water came out of taps into a very deep white enamelled bath. This bath had feet, I could almost swim in it. At home our bath hung on a nail in the yard and was brought in once a week, to be filled by kettles of water, boiled on the fire. When we'd all had a bath, as they say, my dad would empty it with a laden tin and pail into the sink in our yard.

We got off the train at Fencehouses to go to Gram-ma's

Our tap was in the scullery, over a stone slab where we could stand a dish or pail.

I was fascinated by her house, a dormer type bungalow, semi-detached, with a kitchen, complete with gas stove. There was a brick air raid shelter in her front garden. This had to be shared with the old man next door, Lukie Wilson. He was a Bill Sykes look alike, with a patch eyed bull terrier to match. The bathroom with toilet, adjoined the kitchen. Through the kitchen was the living room with a big black range, that you never saw without a good fire going. There was a cosy wooden stool, called a crackett, just around the corner next to the fire. This had a cushion on it and was my favourite seat. A rocking chair sat at the other side of the fireplace, by a little pantry. Gram-ma had a square table with a big rust coloured cover and tassels hanging down around the edge. There was a big sideboard with ornaments and pictures on it. On the wall at each side, there were long mirrors with birds and butterflies on them. The floor was lino, covered with clipping mats. The fireplace shone with black lead polish and the iron hinges on the oven door were kept brightly polished. The fire was placed high up, with the ash box underneath to catch the hot ashes when you poked the fire. Coals were always thrown from a coal bucket onto the fire back, which was a flat shelf behind the fire and below the chimney. Coals were heaped on the fire back and raked forward when required, onto the fire, by means of an iron rake, with a long handle. There was a matching poker and these implements laid on the hearth behind a brass and steel fender, that was always highly polished. Sometimes as you were sitting around the fire, there would be an almighty rumble and banging noise in the back boiler, which would then go gurgling through the pipes to the bathroom. Gram-ma would remark, "Eeh!, the water's boilin'. Just a minute and Ar'll put the dog in". With that she would reach into the fire with the poker, to move the dog, which was an iron plate, with a hole for the poker, used to divert the heat from the boiler. The boiler would soon quieten down to a gentle singing. There was another dog which had to be moved to heat the oven. These were the only dogs she had, mind you, she had a black cat. You can imagine, that cleaning out the flues was an essential weekly chore, to keep everything working properly.

Although there was a gas cooker, there was always a big black sooty kettle on the hob by the fire, which sang away contentedly, in readiness for making a brew of tea at a moments notice. There were also some iron tongs in case you had to lift hot coal from the mat. Now when I first visited gram-ma's, there was Bill, her brother, uncle Roger and aunty Edith, who were children of her second marriage. Having brought up a family of one boy and three girls, she then brought up a second family of two girls and one boy and had also lost twins in infancy. Such were those days, hard times and little money to feed and clothe a family. Gram-ma's brother Bill, was retired, after fifty years down the pit, and lived with her at that time. Sometimes, he would have some of his old marrers round, for a pipe of baccy and a bit crack about old times. They made their own entertainment, perhaps played dominoes.

On the wall above the fireplace was a framed verse:

CHRIST IS THE HEAD OF THIS HOUSE
THE UNSEEN GUEST AT EVERY MEAL
THE SILENT LISTENER TO EVERY CONVERSATION

A kind of good luck omen from a strict protestant upbringing, mainly superstition. The very thought gave me the shivers, like a ghost creeping about, especially when I slept there on a shakey down. The great thrill of staying at gram-ma's, was to sleep on the floor, on some spare bedding and blankets. They called this a shakey down, head to the wall. I used to think that this must be the next best thing to camping outside, which I longed to do, but had to wait many years before I was allowed.

My grandfather had been of Irish origin, from County

A game of dominoes and a bit crack

Sligo in the West of Ireland. He and his brother Jim had emigrated to England during the great potato famine at the turn of the century. The family name was Lougheed, 'Head of the Lough', but this was changed on their arrival in England to Lockhead, more pronouncable and easier to spell, which made sense. These two Irish brothers came to County Durham, when there was work to be had in the booming coal mines. I only know what I learned from my mother about this, which must have been second hand, as her father died when she was six years old. He was buried on the day that my mam's sister Lil was born. What a predicament to be left in, widowed at thirty, with four children. Had he been killed outright, she would have had free coal from the mining company. As it was, he suffered head injuries and died some months later in a lunatic asylum.

His brother Jim didn't enter the coal mines but became a male nurse at Sedgefield Mental Hospital, the asylum as it was known. Jim was not very pleased when his mentally deranged brother was admitted as a patient and must have been relieved when he finally died. Uncle Jim had been very kind to my mam when she'd lost her father, she was a favourite of his.

The two brothers William and Jim, had married two sisters, Elizabeth, my grandmother and Annie. Annie unfortunately died in childbirth and uncle Jim was married for the second time, to aunty Cissie. They took care of my mam and thought a great deal about Bette and me, we had many happy times there.

Uncle Jim's place at Sedgefield, was a large old house on the High Street, with a big garden and smallholding behind. This was really two houses with a linking door between. Their daughter Hilda, lived in the adjoining house with her husband and three boys. Uncle Jim was a man of tremendous energy and would work very hard in his smallholding after returning from his night shift at the asylum. As well as Hilda, they had brought up four sons.

Their smallholding made them almost self sufficient and his country background in County Sligo must have taught him a great deal about this way of life. There were pigs and hens and rows of potatoes and other vegetables as well as flowers. A greenhouse provided lovely tomatoes and there

My Grandparents

was a vine with grapes.

The pigs were favourites of mine, especially when they had litters of piglets. There was a large boiler by the pig sty where all scraps of food, potato peelings and cabbage stalks were mixed together with pig meal from a sack. The whole lot was boiled up into a rich broth for the pigs. They would squeal with delight as they greedily devoured their swill.

People killed their own pigs in those days, but I never saw this happen, only the sides of bacon hanging up on hooks from the kitchen beam. Aunty Cissie would use every part of the animal to produce food, black pudding, trotters, sausages, nothing went to waste. Her home cured bacon and ham had a delicious taste, "This is home fed", she would say proudly, "there's nothing to beat it". The hens were free range and the egg yolks were deep rich yellow. These were real old fashioned farm eggs, with flavour to match the colour. At feeding time she would say, "Come on Brian, you can help me to mix the crowdie, and we'll go up to feed the hens".

From their back yard you had to go up some stone steps to the garden. Half way up there was an earth closet. This was a very interesting 'netty.' There was the traditional wooden seat, like a bench, but this one had two round holes, one large, one small for children, each with its own lift off cover. I was fascinated by this netty, with its vivid pink washed walls, and strong smell of disinfectant. This was always my first port of call when we arrived there.

There were always lots of flies about in the kitchen window and I would spend, what seemed hours trying to kill these, with the help of my half cousins. These flies were so quick that a rubber band was an essential weapon to make any impact. A better fly wanger was a whalebone or spring steel stay from your mam's old corsets. These worked like magic, the poor old flies had no chance, but were forever replaced by the reserves, waiting on the hanging sides of bacon. Uncle Jim always spoke in a loud voice, through shouting at the patients I suppose, but he was kind and generous. It's funny, they always called my mam, Viley, no one else did, a pet name for her, from childhood. She always returned home, bearing gifts of tomatoes, apples,

My first port of call – the netty

potatoes, eggs and flowers. I think uncle Jim was trying to make up for her losing her father at the tender age of six. Sometimes I would sit at the tea table with my mug of tea up to my face. He would frighten me by suddenly shouting, "Get that pot down!". This made me jump and spill my tea. "Oh leave him alone Jim", aunty Cissie would intervene, "he doesn't know you're joking". Then he would laugh, "It's all right pet, you wear your gas mask if you like". I always kept an eye on him after that, when I was drinking my tea.

CHAPTER 8

HAWKERS

As well as the normal delivery men and club men, there were hawkers, rag and bone men and gypsy women regularly to be seen in our back streets. We learned from parents' chat, that there was a Hanratty involved in this business of collecting rags and bones and other rubbish. There was an old woman with black hair tied back tight and a hawkish weather beaten face. She would come around, sack on back opening back gates and shouting, "Scowrin – scowry stones, scowrin – scowry stones" that was her only cry. She was offering pieces of white chalk like stone, scouring stones, for scouring your front step edges, to make them look smart. Most working class folks that had a front step, would keep the edge white and scoured as they kept their kitchen ranges shining black, they took a pride in their homes. To the best of my knowledge, the only source of the scouring stone, was the hawkers. They soon wore down with use and needed replacement, all you needed were rags or old clothes that were unsuitable for clipping mats. Anyway, to us bairns, this old scowry woman must be the Ann Ratty we heard about, seemed logical. It was only years later that I discovered that Hanratty was a scrap dealer who received the collectings of the hawkers and gypsies for cash payment. We used to run and hide when Ann Ratty appeared in our back street, I think she had an evil eye.

Let me tell you about the Beetroot Man, as we youngsters knew him. A regular caller, around the back streets was an old man, who stooped, had dirty unkempt hair, a three day beard, and a dirty face. This man was enveloped in a dirty, greasy, raincoat, that hung from his drooping shoulders. He wore wellington boots with tops turned down, so that they looked like half wellies. Whatever the weather, rain, snow or shine, his outfit was the same, with a dirty white silk muffler around his neck, tucked into his raincoat, which was buttoned up to the neck. Over his slightly humped back and drooping shoulders he carried a big hessian sack. We listened to his cry, many times as children and there was no doubt whatsoever that he had beetroot for sale, in his sack. His cry was, "Beetroot, beetroot", then again, "Beetroot, beetroot", like a cracked record. He always was and always will be the beetroot man to me, although I learned much later that his cry was "Beg-bones – beg-bones".

When the war got under way, there was a big campaign by the government to collect iron and steel to be used in the manufacture of munitions. There was a fenced compound made at the edge of the allotments, at the end of Oxford Street, near us. This compound was used for old pots and pans and empty tins that people were encouraged to save, to beat Hitler. Our contribution to the war effort, was to go around people's houses nearby, collecting empty tins to throw onto the dump. Iron railings were cut off at their roots by a man wearing dark goggles and using a blow torch. No matter whose house or garden wall, all railings fell to this reaper of iron, with his relentless blowtorch. It was thrilling to watch the white sparks flying as the fierce torch burned through the iron railings, leaving only stumps in their leaded sockets, set in the stone walls. That our tin cans would be used to kill Germans, was reward enough to us English Patriots.

Once when I was ill with mumps I recall, I was in my bed in the kitchen and don't remember feeling so poorly as I did then. "Our Brian's poorly" my mam would tell callers, "we've put his bed in the kitchen, so that Ar can keep an eye on him". I would be gazing at the kitchen window, into the back yard and from my position could only see the sky through the taped panes of glass. The taping was advised by the Air Raid Warden, to prevent flying glass in an air raid. My dad also made shutters from wood laths and roofing felt, which were put over the outside of the windows at night to maintain the blackout.

One day I began to feel better, as I laid there and gazed at the clouds floating by. My heart leaped for joy when I heard the back gate sneck, then my dad's whistle, as he came into the yard. He always gave a whistle as he came home from work, just two notes, to announce his arrival. He looked through the window with a big smile and waved. I felt so happy that he'd come home and was pleased that I was improving. "Look what A'rve got Brian", he said, as he took a brown paper bag from his bait bag. Something was moving inside. He opened the bag and there was a beautiful yellow canary crouching in the corner. Unbeknown to me, he had made a wooden birdcage, painted green with metal bars and a little swinging door. This was soon fixed on the wall and was to be the home for Dick, our canary. Dick seemed pleased to be out of the bag and hopped around from perch to perch, singing as he went. Two little troughs of white boodie were clipped onto the inside of the bars. These provided water and birdseed. The bottom of the cage, which slid out for cleaning, was covered with a thin layer of fine sand, which reminded me of seaside sand. I was very thrilled to have our first family pet, that I could help to look after. My mam soon made a cage cover from some spare curtain material, for night time – to keep out the draughts.

For some reason, my mam and dad had to go away somewhere overnight and I was to stay at Mr and Mrs Brown's house, two doors down from us. They had two boys, Ronnie and Eric, both older than me. This was a great adventure, going to sleep in their bedroom. We all were to share the same bed. After our supper, we all got our pyjamas on downstairs and off we went up to bed. "Before we go to bed" said Ronnie, "we have to kneel at the bedside – you go first." They pushed me through the door. My dad had always taught me to say my prayers before going to sleep,

but usually in bed, not kneeling, but some people knelt,
like in church. I knelt by the bed and closed my eyes, with
hands together. "Gentle Jesus, meek and mild, look upon a
little child, God bless Mammy and Daddy and Bette and
make me a good boy – amen." I got up and went to the
door. "Finished?" said Ronnie, "Now you Eric". Eric went in
next. When he came out he said, "Oh didn't you want one
Brian?" I was puzzled, until Ronnie went in, he wasn't
bashfull and left the door open. Down he went on his knees
and pulled out a large white chamber pot, a poe we called
it and got a weewee, before pushing it back under the bed.
Not a single word of prayer was uttered. That was the one
and only occasion I stayed at the Browns' house, but I had
learned what to do another time, if I was invited to stay
again.

Although the back street was cobbled, the road at the
top where you went around the end houses to the front
streets was just made of earth or dirt as we knew it, there
were vertical wooden railings, the rec boundary. One of
these was missing and you could take a short cut into the
rec, through long grass and then to the sand pit and
swings.

The dirt was compressed, through being walked on, ideal
for playing marbles or pop allies as we knew them. You
could easily make holes to shoot the allies into or make
tracks to run your Dinky cars along. There was sometimes,
a very tall boy who would come along that way, to the rec,
he was from several streets away, a foreigner. I know he
was tall because he would stand on his tiptoes and look
over the railings into the rec. He was a rough type and
everything was a, "Bliddy this" or "bliddy that". My mam
said that he was swearing and I should come straight
home when he appeared. I used to see this boy in later
years, when he was grown into a man. The only thing I
ever remembered about him was his "Bliddy" swear word.

It may have been when my aunty Edith stayed, when
our baby arrived or it may have been another time when
she took me to the rec. There were some swings and rings,
a teapot lid and a sand pit near to our gate when I would
go to play with my pals. Further into the rec, there were
some bigger swings, an ocean wave, a teapot lid and a

slide, also a paddling pool. This is where Edith took me. I'll never forget that trip, as it ended unhappily for me. I wanted to go to the lav, when there was no lav and filled my pants, as they say. Poor aunty Edith held my hand and walked me slowly back home, crying and saying repeatedly – "Papa, papa", people knew I wasn't crying for my dad. She would only be fourteen years old at the time and must have suffered great embarrassment. No doubt she would be pleased to hand me over to her big sister, to get me sorted out and washed down. The tale was often told over in the family, usually by my dad, accompanied by guffaws of laughter from all.

Aunty Edith must have been a glutton for punishment, because on a later occasion she took me again to the rec, this time to the paddling pool. The rec keeper or groundsman was Mr Snailham. Old Snail-Eye we called him. The paddling pool was circular and went from six inches to something like sixteen inches deep. At the start of the summer, Snail-Eye would clean out the dry pool and turn the water on, to fill it for the season. The filling of the pool was an exciting occasion, the water squirted from a pipe at the edge and made hisses and splashes until the pool was filled. Edith and me both took off our shoes and socks and left them on the grass. In we went, hand in hand, what a thrill, almost like the seaside, only the water was warmer. It was just right, up to my knees in water, until I was bumped by someone, lost my balance and fell over backwards. I was sure my end had come, coughing and spluttering. What a shock on my system, Edith walked me home like a drowned rat, this time wailing, "Mammy, mammy".

When my dad got his secondhand bike. People would say to him, "Bah, that's a canny bike Fred, is it a three speeder?" "No" he would reply with a laugh, "it's one of those – you know, the faster you pedal, the faster it goes". Then they would laugh. This bike was used for going to and from work. Sometimes I would meet him at the bottom of the back street. He would lift me onto the saddle and let me hold the handlebars. Being pushed up the back street to our gate was always a thrill and a treat for me, with the sound of the ticking free wheel under me and the bell that I could reach and ring to my heart's content. Something

Edith, my favourite Aunty

went wrong with my dad's bike, a sprocket or something and it was no longer rideable, he could pedal, the chain went round, but didn't turn the rear wheel. This had me really puzzled and him also. Clever as he was, he had the wheel all to pieces, but something was broken that he could not mend. The bike was not a Raleigh or anything so grand, but a CWS, made at the Cooperative Wholesale Society's bicycle factory in Newcastle. Not Byker !!

It was a joke amongst local folks, many who worked for the store, that CWS stood for, Copper Wire and String! What a reputation for the Coop! He took his bike back to the store, in Newgate Street. It had to be sent away, to be repaired. Because of the war, there were no spare parts to be had, or so he was informed after several weeks of waiting. "Well you may as well keep it", he told them. So the bike went for scrap. He walked to work after that. There were no bikes to be had, even if he had the money to buy one! Never mind the bike, some dads went away to the war and never came back, how lucky I was that my dad had a reserved occupation, which prevented him from being called up to go to fight the Germans.

He had trained to be part of the emergency team, that could be sent, at a moment's notice, to deal with and make safe, live underground cables, in towns and cities that had been bombed. They had special trucks, with all necessary equipment to carry out these tasks. The London Blitz was a ferocious and unrelenting attack by the Luftwaffe, that lasted for forty days. His team were next in line, when the raids stopped, as abruptly as they had begun.

On the underground electrical distribution network, there were installed numerous inspection points to access cables in the ground. In the event of a German invasion, his team were to hammer steel spikes through the cables to shut down the network and confuse the enemy.

Another friend of mine, Billy Walker, lived further down the street. Well, his dad was in the RAF, for when he came home on leave, he wore a uniform and airman's cap. Knicknamed Banty Walker, because of his small stature. Just a little stocky man but noted for his ability to sink pints of beer, which he did when he was on leave and no doubt when he wasn't on leave. The story goes that Mrs

Walker was friendly with another man, whilst Banty was away, doing his bit for King and Country. Children hear grown-ups talking, as they play around on the floor and remember. So I learned that Banty had arrived home unexpectedly one day, on leave, to find his wife entertaining her boyfriend. The outcome was that Banty gave him the boot, then gave her a good hiding. They said, "By Jove, he's only a little bloke, but what a temper". This story was told over more than once as you can imagine. Such goings on!

Before the blackout, the streets of Bishop were lit by gaslight. There was a lamp-post in our street. Just before dusk, Lenny Harburn the lamplighter would appear at the bottom of the street. He wore an overcoat and a trilby hat and carried a long pole over his shoulder. At the top of the pole was a hook and a winking oil flame from a wick inside the pole. His first move was to turn on the gas by hooking a lever under the lantern, the hiss of gas followed, in went the pole, through a little trapdoor and, pop, the gas mantle

A job for Lenny – Lighting up the town

was lit, giving off a warm white light, a friendly light. I would follow him to the next street when he repeated the performance.

When everyone was in bed, he would go round again, turning out the lights around the town. With the blackout, the street lights were never lit again 'til after the war. Then Lenny re-emerged from his long 'harburnation', to continue where he left off, lighting up the town, as though there had never been a war on.

CHAPTER 9

TIME SLIP

My mam was always running behind schedule, especially when we had a bus or a train to catch. She managed time in the same way as she managed money – badly. Nevertheless she had an ingenious solution to the problem of missing buses and trains. You might imagine that she got out of bed ten minutes earlier, set off to the station ten minutes earlier and so on. That was not her way, her way was much simpler. Our clock, which stood on the sideboard, was always set ten minutes fast! As a youngster learning to tell the time, this caused me some problems as you can imagine. The only other clock that we had access to, was on the tower of Wesley Chapel, in Newgate Street. By looking out of our front door, we could see one of the four faces of Wesley clock, which always kept perfect time, as this was wound up and tended to, every week by my dad. So I learned to read two kinds of time, Wesley Clock, which was the same as they gave off on the wireless, and our sideboard clock which was ten minutes fast.

A further refinement was added, to save another minute, this was for my mam to send me on ahead to hold the bus for her. If we were heading for the market place to catch the bus to my gram-ma's, the final straight, down Bondgate was always at a trot, with me ahead by a hundred yards or so. The bus drivers kindly obliged. "All right pet", when I said, "Could you wait a minute please? mam's just coming." They knew her well. With the railway station, this was more difficult, but she banked on the reputation of the driver, to be also running behind schedule. Hence we rarely missed a train, but it was often a near thing. I would still go ahead, across the rec and stand on the footbridge over the railway line. From there I could see her appear from a great distance, running, arriving rosy cheeked, panting and out of breath. She went home, as she said, regularly to see her mother, taking me and my sister with her, whilst my dad was at work. We never had a problem with missing buses on the return journey as my grandmother would say, "Yer'd better go now Vi or yer'll miss your bus." Imposed discipline. It worked.

My dad was a cable jointer. He was often to be found in a hole in the road, sitting on a three legged milking type stool placed on a rubber mat. Here he would practice his highly skilled craft on a live underground cable. Great care and patience were of the essence, as one false move could result in electrocution and death. He was a well known and popular man in the district through his travelling around as a local preacher and was often interrupted in his work by friends and aquaintances who stopped to say hello. Interruption was the last thing he needed when making live connections or pouring molten solder from a ladle onto the cable joint. There was always a tent with a green tarpaulin and two large tool boxes that doubled up as seats, all the accoutrements of his trade were strewn around, blowlamps, paraffin, tins of cotton tape immersed in oil, to be applied like bandages. There was lead sleeving to be fashioned and dressed into shape by means of wooden lead beaters, there was tallow and plumbers black. Always there was a glowing coke brazier for heating the pots of solder and plumbing metal, not to mention the big black iron kettle that sat nudging up the brazier, singing all day and ever ready to make a brew of tea, which was consumed by the gallon by the jointing gang. The bottoms of my dad's overalls, invariably displayed patches and burns. There were usually two or three paraffin blowlamps going and it was not unknown for him to get too near and set his overall legs afire. Little wisps of singed curling hairs on his fingers and wrists, bore evidence of the scorches of the roaring blowlamp flame that plied them on a regular basis. There was a small mirror with a brass frame that he used for checking the underside of the joint. It was fascinating to see him work with blowlamp, wiper, mirror, tallow and all the rest. He used to tell people that he was like a surgeon, all his mistakes were buried. Joking apart, most of his best works of art were buried in the ground. All of this gave my dad a very distinctive smell, like a subtle blend of perfume. The ingredients were paraffin, fluxite, tallow, oil, pitch and coke, the proportions were a strict secret, just like 4711 Cologne. A pleasant, manly smell, without a trace of tobacco, as he never succumbed to the weed. This was my dad, the cleverest man in the world to me. There was no job he couldn't do, my priorities had changed. All I wanted to be was a cable jointer like him.

Another skill, for which he was renowned was cutting hair. This skill was perfected after many years of practice on my curly locks. I always sported a mop of golden curls until I started school, whereupon the order of the day, was the then fashionable, short back and sides. As my dad's skill improved, the ridges became less pronounced with ensuing haircuts, not that anyone minded, most boys' haircutting was a bit rough, even by the barber.

The local barber was Harry Nawson, along Etherley Lane towards the Town Head. He was always known as, Dog Harry, but never to his face. As lads, we always imagined that this was because he trimmed dogs in his spare time. It was not until many years later that I found that the reason for the nickname, was that Harry was fond of betting on the dogs, local greyhound races. Sometimes when my hair was getting long and unruly, my dad would say, "Ar think you'd better go to see Dog Harry and have a proper haircut". Often I heard men say as they sat in his barber's chair, "Don't take much off Harry". The request fell on deaf ears, Harry knew best. He specialised in short back and sides, that was his one and only style. "Oh, thoo wants plenty off lad," he would remark, as his shears buzzed up into their crop, well past the ears. When he'd done, a liberal dollop of Brylcream was well rubbed in,

Bow-Wow Brooch

before combing and brushing. I must say his customers were turned out to an immaculate standard, to make the most beady eyed RSM throw his chest out and bristle with pride.

There was a popular song in the forties, 'Daddy Wouldn't Buy Me a Bow-Wow'. This was my party piece, taught to me by my dad. It went like this –

> *Daddy wouldn't buy me a bow-wow*
> *Daddy wouldn't buy me a bow-wow*
> *I've got a little cat and I'm very fond of that*
> *But I'd rather have a bow-wow-wow!*

But the only bow-wows I possessed, were a little scottie dog brooch in my beret and a Bonzo ornament, which stood on our sideboard.

I learned to recite nursery rhymes and little ditties that my dad would sing. He had started in the pit as a wagon way lad, so his song was appropriate, 'Down The Wagon Way! He sang as he sat me on his knee, clapping my hands together.

> *Clap your hands for daddie's comin'*
> *Down the wagon way*
> *A penny in his pocket*
> *For his little boy today* – then he would sing,

> *Wee baby bunting*
> *Daddie's gone a hunting*
> *To get a little rabbit skin*
> *To wrap his baby bunting in* – followed by,

> *You shall have a fishie*
> *In a little dishie*
> *You shall have a bloater*
> *When the boat comes in.*

Oh happy days – what bliss!

CHAPTER 10

SCHOOL

Easter 1940 was my first day at school, my teacher was a lovely dark haired, kindly lady called Miss Bruce. To me, Miss Bruce was like a film star, a real smasher. She was in charge of the first class at Etherley Lane Council School, just five minutes walk from our house, through the rec. My mam took me along that first morning, complete with gas mask, which everyone was obliged to carry at all times in case Hitler dropped gas bombs on us. Fortunately we were too young to appreciate the gravity of the situation, but our parents must have had great anxieties about the future, in those troubled days.

The headmaster of our school was Mr Siddle, a brutish looking bespectacled man with short cropped hair and a ruddy face, not unlike Heinrich Himmler. A man to be feared and respected, he ruled his little charges with booming voice, the cane, and the occasional boxed ear. Nobody stepped out of line when he was around. Having said that, none of our teachers were backward in dispensing the cane. I was terrified of Mr Siddle on sight, his manner, the way he spoke, with short clipped sentences. I was glad my mam was with me, when I had to go to his office to register.

Miss Bruce created discipline by keeping our noses to

the grindstone, together with kindly encouragement. Unlike some children, I managed not to shed tears on my first day at school. My friend Arthur, cried so much that his mother was sent for, to take him home. Next day he was alright, he had overcome the initial shock of being left by his mother. We learned to recite the alphabet and our multiplication tables. This was done relentlessly day after day, we learned the three R's, by the time tested methods of rote. There were no trendy teachers in those days.

The classroom was always cosy and warm in winter and Mr Bramwell, the peg legged caretaker would come clonking around to the radiators, squirting air and hot water into a tin jug that he carried. The school was spotlessly clean and smelled of nothing but polish and chalk, although some of the children were far from sweet smelling. Those from the Town Head, a poor slum area often came to school dirty. I mean dirt that was set in, as we would say, clothes were ragged and malodorous, boots and shoes had gaping holes, with no socks. There was a regular morning parade of certain boys to the washroom, cold water only and green bar soap, most of the dirt finished up on the coarse roller towels which Mr Bramwell changed on a daily rota. These youngsters brought head lice, impetigo and ringworm and often had parts of their heads shaved, sporting dabs of iodine or gentian violet. These maladies soon spread to other children, as we were all in close proximity.

On one occasion I was off school with impetigo, my face was covered in scabs, painted with gentian violet to dry and heal them. I was playing on my own, swinging around the lamp post in our street, when I looked down, I couldn't believe my eyes, there was a pound note, lying at my feet. I took it home with great rejoicing to my mam. "Bah!, what a lucky find Brian, Ar wonder where that came from. Go and see if you can find any more". But there were no more.

There were epidemics of head lice which I would catch at school. If I was scratching my head, my mam would remark, "Brian, Ar think you must have nits, you're always scratchin' ". Sure enough, she would locate them by inspection and combing with a fine toothed comb. The adults, she called creepers and were killed by washing with Derbac soap. This did not however destroy the clusters of eggs on the scalp. These were the nits. My mam was very adept at combing these out, onto a sheet of brown paper, whereupon she would crack them between her thumbnails. That was the end of them – until the next time!

There were boys and girls from the Cottage Homes at our school. These were orphans. The homes, were provided by the London and North Eastern Railway Company, LNER. These children were spotlessly clean and dressed in drab grey uniform. Grey trousers and skirts, grey shirts and blouses, grey socks, with black boots and shoes. They were institutionalised children, well behaved and apparently a bit thick in the head. They were often reminded of this, by some of our unfeeling teachers.

I was shy, especially during my early days at school. If you wanted a pencil, or wanted to go to the toilet, you had to raise your hand. I saw others do it, but had a great dread of having to ask the teacher for anything and kept my head well down, hoping not to be noticed. There was one morning, I felt a great urge to visit the lavatory and in the end, sheer desperation forced me to put my hand up. "Yes Brian, what is it?" asked Miss Bruce. "Please miss Ar want to go to the lavatory". "All right, off you go" she responded. Next big problem! I remembered my mam always fastened the back buttons on my braces. "Please miss, Ar can't fasten me braces backs". "Oh, then Arthur can go with you. Now you go with Brian, Arthur to help him with his braces". As she was saying these words, I quietly passed wind, bringing instant relief. My great urge, disappeared. "But Ar don't want to go yet miss", I said with my new found relief. "You'd better go back to your desk then", said Miss Bruce. She took it all in her stride, "Now we're going to recite our tables".

For some reason I was never able to understand, my mam got me shoes, with a strap across, fixed by a button. Also, some of my coats were buttoned right over left like a girl's, they may have been secondhand. This was soon noticed and the other boys and girls would make fun of me. "Lassie lad, lassie lad", they would call, I wished I could hide away somewhere, but there was nowhere to hide. I didn't want to be different from everyone else, my mam was insensitive in that respect. Sometimes I wondered if she had really wanted a girl, I knew that my hair was parted on the right, and always wanted to go that way, but she may have encouraged it to do so. It took little to embarrass me. On one occasion I discovered to my horror that my pullover was inside out. Before anyone noticed, I dropped my pencil on the floor and was soon underneath the desk, taking off my pullover and changing it around. This was not very easy in a confined space. "What are you doing rummaging under that desk Brian ?", enquired Miss Bruce. I had just made it, "Please miss Ar was just lookin' for me pencil". "Alright, now everybody get your counters out for adding up". Then we would empty the little tins of coloured cardboard circles onto our desks. We had a matching tin for plasticine, with its distinctive smell.

During my first year at school, there was a girl by the name of Anne Jenkinson, I think she started school after the summer holiday, whereas I had started at Easter. She lived in a house, very near to the school, what we would call, a posh house, semi-detached with a garden. I thought that Anne was very special and imagined that she was my sweetheart. She had the most wonderful smell of flowers, this must have been perfume and was a smell that I had never encountered before. This attracted me to the extent that I would love to smell her coat, when I hung mine in the cloakroom. If my mam had known, she would have been extremely concerned that I was taking the first steps on that slippery slope to the depths of depravity. Anne wasn't there long, her parents sent her to private school and who could blame them!

The teaching standards in Etherley Lane School were abysmal, very few of the teachers knew the first thing about communicating with children. My dad said that they were only trainees and not proper teachers. Their methods were those of intimidation, bellowing and bullying, they rarely produced a single eleven plus exam pass. They were bottom of the league. This is where I received my basic educational grounding.

At playtime, we all poured out into the school yard. A whistle was blown to signal going into school or the end of playtime. On hearing this whistle, we were to stand perfectly still until commanded, "Get in your lines", followed by the second whistle. Once aligned in neat rows, we were commanded, "Right turn, by the left – quick march", whereupon Miss Bruce would strike up a vigorous marching tune on the piano, which was just inside the wide open doors into the school. 'Blaze Away', was her favourite tune, as we marched in orderly lines into our classrooms. We always started the day with assembly in the large hall, a hymn and a prayer. When we had prayers, we stood with our hands together under our chins, with eyes closed.

It was widely believed by myself and others, that if you peeped during prayers, you might see an angel. Nobody dared to peep, in case God struck them down with his 'terrible swift sword'. I never saw the sword in action, but I do remember once, that a boy by the name of Norman Gornell was ear boxed to the ground by the 'terrible swift hand' of the headmaster, because he ventured to open his eyes during the Lord's Prayer. We all opened our eyes at that point

We all had free milk

and never questioned as to how Mr Siddle had seen Norman peeping, through his closed eyelids. Perhaps he was 'all seeing', like God, this wonderful, loving and caring God that we read about in the Bible. Even to small children, this kind of treatment didn't ring true. I often wondered whether Norman became a staunch believer and if Mr Siddle believed in God. Our first lesson every morning was Scripture Study, when we were read stories from the Bible.

There was a Jewish boy in our class called John Goldstein, he had a strange accent, I think from London, his mother used to say things like, "Oh that's awfully nice" and other such phrases, that were completely foreign to us. John was excused scripture because he was not a Christian and just read a book instead. We thought this strange. I got on well with him and sometimes was invited round to his house to play, in Clarence Street,not far away. As bairns, we were confused about the war and who was on whose side. My visits to the Goldsteins' home, didn't go unnoticed by the other lads in our street. "Hey Jossie", they would accuse, "why are you friends with that German Jew?". There had been so much talk of Germans and German Jews on the wireless, they were all the same to us. I had to think quickly to get out of this jam. "Ar'm just goin' around there to spy on them", I volunteered, "to get to know their plans." This completely satisfied these young patriots and my bacon was saved once more.

CHAPTER 11

MOVING

In 1941 when I was six, we moved to another rented house which had two bedrooms and a cellar under the sitting room. This house belonged to Mr Wood who lived in Etherley Lane. The rent was three shillings a week, which was paid in cash and entered in a Rent Book. There was great excitement when mam and dad took Bette and me to look around this house, which was at the top side of the school, just two doors from the school yard. The previous occupants had moved out, when we visited and this gave us a lot of freedom to explore. There was a back yard with a coalhouse and lavatory. Immediately behind us was the water tower for the town, being the highest point. This was a well known landmark and could be seen for miles around. There was a whitewashed pantry with wooden shelves, and a slatted window with a perforated zinc fly screen. This adjoined the scullery as my mam called it, a relic of her days in service. Some people would call this their back kitchen. Living room was not a term which we used. We lived in the kitchen, which had a black fireplace and oven range for cooking and a floor of damp and uneven stone flags. The sitting room at the front of the house was known as, the front room or simply, 'the room'.

The scullery had a brass cold tap on the wall, over a

stone slab, where you stood your pail or dish to get water. There was no sink or drain. The drain was in the back yard, where you emptied all dirty water from your slop pail. A passage from the front door lead to the stairs. The room, was off the passage, very posh wood boarded floor and a fireplace. We had an electric light in each room except the cellar. There was a candle skewered onto a nail behind the lavatory door, for when it was dark. The cellar was pure magic, with its wooden beams and stone flagged floor. A window looked out to beneath a grating in the pavement. This could be slid open for ventilation and I found two pennies there that someone had lost down the grating. A gas meter ticked on the cellar wall, next to a gas oven, with its greasy dank smell of coal gas and burned dripping. The only oven we'd had before, was heated by the fire. "Bah, what a grand oven, it just needs a good clean, Ar can make some grand Yorkshire puddin's in that" said mam. I was to have my own bedroom at the back, looking out onto the water tower. Bette was still in her cot which would go in the front bedroom with mam and dad.

The next thing I knew, was that we were moving to our new house in Lindsay Street and I travelled in the cab of the open backed removal lorry, with the driver and my dad. The day was warm and sunny as the lorry chugged away up our new street. It pulled up at the second house from the top on the left hand side, by a dark green door with a black letterbox and number 21 to match.

There were some boys about my age, sitting chalking on the pavement nearby. They were curious about the arrival of this new family and soon spotted me sitting up in the cab. I felt so clever, in that high position behind the steering wheel. Whilst my dad and the driver carried our furniture into the house, I climbed in and out of the cab, through the open window just showing off to these boys and making them laugh. They were to become my new pals and were soon in the cab with me, having a go at driving by swinging the steering wheel from side to side. By this time my mam appeared at the bottom of the street, pushing Bette in her pram. She had walked and brought a few of the remaining odds and ends, piled on the pram.

"Bah, we're choking for a drink of tea", said my dad,

"Ar'm glad you've brought the kettle". Soon we were settled down with pots of tea all round.

"Ar think Ar'll go for some fish and chips for our dinners", said mam. We all agreed, that was a good idea, so off she went. What an ending to a perfect day, moving house, riding in a lorry, new found friends, fish and chips, my own bedroom, this exceeded all my dreams.

How lucky I was, even if there was a war on, they never did ration fish and chips. These were the staple diet of most working class families and made a fortune for the fish shops. They were open every day except Sunday. No shops opened on a Sunday.

There was always a queue in the fish shop, of which there were many around the town. The nearest one to us was Scotts. They didn't sell wet fish, only fried fish, fried in golden batter, with chips. Salt and vinegar were the only condiments and these stood on the counter, with a shining but greasy brass hand rail along its front. Small children, especially boys, for which the rail was at mouth height, would swing on it with their grubby hands and suck it as they waited impatiently for their turn to be served. Running noses were not uncommon.

Behind the counter was our Sunday School superintendent, Mr Scott with a broad smile and curly hair, wearing a white coat. He kept disappearing into the back and re-emerging with trays of fish, which he dipped in turn into a tray of white batter, before slipping them into the hot fat, with a hiss.

There were young women sitting, permanently peeling and eyeing potatoes – and eyeing any young men, that appeared in the queue. What a life! Then there was the Chief Chip Chopper, placing the white and clean potatoes, long way up under this fearsome guillotine like machine. Then with one mighty pull of the handle, the deed was done. Fresh raw chips, oozing starch, dropped into the waiting white enamelled pail beneath. The trick was to get your fingers out of the way before the ram descended. Many a slick chip chopper, fell foul to the guillotine and was able to give the boy scouts salute without folding his pinky. Mr Scott was a wizard, with all the frying, tending and taking money – the washing of hands was a rarity!

Sizzling hot fish and chips were deposited into tiny paper bags, token bags they were. It must have been the shortage of paper. The majority spilled out into the outer wrapping of newspaper. Newspapers were stacked in a great pile on the counter end, ready for wrapping. Where they came from we knew not, their dubious history we knew not, where they had been was anybody's guess. What with the sucking rail and newspapers, we grew immune to diseases which are prevalent in the affluent society. The fish shop was a major factor in boosting our immune systems. There was a saying, a bit of muck does you good, which had a great element of truth in it.

We soon got settled into our new house and my dad wired a light in the cellar and fixed up my swing onto a roof beam. The people who moved into our old house must have wondered about the two charred holes in the pantry door frame. The swing in the cellar acted like a magnet to my pals and for yet unborn generations. Not only could you swing to and fro, you could swing in circles, when you launched yourself off my dad's big toolbox which stood by the wall, next to the swing.

This swing was unique amongst all the swings of the world, it creaked and resounded amongst the rafters as you swung back and forth. The wooden seat was just the right size and shape, better than those in the rec. It had nice thick ropes to hold, not cold chains. You could swing for hours on end and time stood still, while you dreamed your dreams away. Bing used to sing, "You could be swinging on a star". I think the swing that my dad made was something like that, a dreamy swing, hypnotic in its rhythms.

In school, we had regular air raid drill, when we all had to lie on the floor under the desks. Sometimes we had to put our gas masks on, when the teacher told us. We all thought this was a lot of fun. Better than lessons. There was great excitement, when a large part of the school field was dug up, to build air-raid shelters. These works were done by a gang of men with wheelbarrows, picks and shovels, who, first of all dug some great big pits in the ground, just outside our classrooms.

The shelters were built of brick and recessed into the ground. They had steps down into them and a concrete roof. All then were covered with mounds of earth, which eventually became covered with grass and weeds, a natural camouflage. When the shelters were complete, we had practice air-raids, when we all had to file out in an orderly mannner, to our allocated places in the shelters. A teacher was in charge of each shelter, one for each class and was equipped with enough wooden benches for thirty or so children. They were dark and damp, with no electricity. Lighting was by two lanterns with candles, fixed to the wall, which the teacher lit, before the large solid wood door was closed.

A thick canvas curtain screen hung inside of the door to stop the light from being seen by German aeroplanes, when the door was used. Somebody was given the job of turning the handle on a machine to ventilate the shelter. This was great excitement and we enjoyed the weekly ritual. Gas masks were always at the ready but fortunately, we were never bombed or gassed.

When there were any workmen around, at school, or working in the street, they always knocked on our door, to ask if my mam would scald their tea for them at bait time, offering cans and tins of tea. She would say jokingly, "Bah, yer never go to the top house, always me, second down, Ar must be well known. Ar'll give a shout when it's mast". The men would just laugh, "Wi man, you're famous for makin' a good brew pet". She was so kind, a bit of a softie, would even use her own tea from our rations. "Eeh thanks pet", they would say, "yer'll get yer reward in heaven".

When all the digging was finished the gang of workmen moved to the rec, where they dug a long deep trench by the hedge, for people to shelter from air-raids. Fortunately it was never needed and became a great adventure playground, where you could play soldiers or use as a convenience.

My dad fixed up some shelves and a workbench out of two old doors. The cellar was to become a laboratory, a melting and mixing pot for budding scientists and engineers. To make it cosy my dad put down bits of spare lino, bits of carpet and old clipping mats on the stone flagged floor. Home from home it was.

Sometimes, if one of my pals came to call for me to go

out, my mam would say, "Oh, Brian's just havin' his tea, would yer like to wait down the cellar"? Would they not! Donald lived across the other side of our street. Like myself, Donnie as he was nicknamed, had no aspirations of becoming anything in life. He was at the same school as me, need I say more?

Despite the pathetic teaching standards, Donnie had a great leaning towards science, especially chemistry, which seemed to fascinate him, although this was not a school subject at Etherley Lane School. We had acquired an old aluminium egg poaching pan, in which we would boil mixtures of leaves and berries, experimenting, to make stinks.

The boiling was done over the flame of candles, usually by the water tower wall, in the back street. Moth balls were also great favourites and readily available from Woolworths. They produced a foul smelling black camphorated smoke, as they burned.

Whilst he was waiting for me in the cellar, swinging, my Mam would remark, "Eeh, what a noise that boy makes, yer'd think there was a dozen down there". Donnie chattered away to himself, living out his fantasies as he swung to and fro, to and fro, creak, creak, creak, chatter, chatter, chatter, laughter, laughter, laughter, dreaming, dreaming of laboratories, with test tubes, thistle funnels, retorts bubbling and hissing. A scientist was evolving from a small boy with a bent for chemistry.

I shall never forget, Donnie would get too excited to leave the cellar to go to the lavatory. For some reason of diet or whatever, his stools were hard balls, like a sheep. With short trousers, he simply reached up his trouser leg and dropped a few into his hand, to be deposited in a dark unused cellar fireplace. Perfectly clean and hygenic. My Mam would shout down to him, "Would yer like a jam sandwich Donald?" "Oh yes please", he was always hungry. Hands were never washed. "Bah, he's as thin as a rake" my Mam would remark, "Ar think he must have worms."

Besides Donnie, there was Howard and Arnie who were also pals of mine, then Carl who lived at the bottom of the street in the terrace next to Mrs Chisholm's shop.

Now Mrs Chisholm was an old lady who had a shop in the front room of her house. The shop window was an ordi-

nary sash window like the others, except it had a small display area, enclosed with a short curtain around it. Jars of
sweets were displayed in the window, boxes of loose
sweets, torpedoes, spanish and so on. Then an assortment
of tins of baking powder, boot polish, shoe laces, cigarettes
of various brands. If you were unlucky, the sweets you
wanted, were in the window.

Mrs Chisholm would slowly and deliberately come
around from behind the counter to the window. She would
carefully open the curtains on their brass rail and reach in,
for the appropriate jar. Then back around the counter and
careful weighing on the scales, usually two ounces, then
into a small pointed paper packet. Back she would trundle
to return the jar to its rightful place and re-adjust the
curtain.

"Right, now let's see, was there anything else?" she
would enquire. "No, well that'll be thre'pence ha'peny and
two coupons please. Thank you". Over the door, hanging
inside the glass fan-light and facing out, was a printed sign
on a piece of faded grey cardboard. MRS CHISHOLM –
GENERAL PROVISIONS. Because of the display window,
the little shop was dark and a light was always needed.
There was no electricity. A swan necked gas bracket from
the Victorian era, provided a gentle warm light from its
glowing mantle. An etched glass shade, sprinkled chinks of
light to every corner of the room, as the gas hissed and
spluttered.

This was not like the bright white electric lamp in our
kitchen, but a living flame, an essential ingredient in the
character of the little shop. Coal gas had the same homely,
welcoming smell, that you got from an open coal fire. As
you entered the shop, there was a bell on a coiled spring,
that clicked and rang, swinging from side to side. It still
rang for several clangs after you shut the door behind you.
Jutting across the shop was a wooden counter with a
Cadbury's Chocolate display cabinet on it.

At the rear of the counter stood Mrs Chisholm, by the
scales, all neat and pin tidy. There were shelves on the
wall behind the counter, displaying all manner of foods
that any household may need.

A magnificent bevelled edged mirror reflected the room

from behind the shelves, making the room look twice its size. The picture of a bearded smoking sailor, adorned the mirror, with the words, Players Navy Cut, emblazoned across it in blue and gold lettering.

On the floor on this side of the counter was a hessian sack, already open, with its polo neck rolled back, to display the potatoes. There were lemonade crates made of wood, orange coloured with, JONES MINERAL WATERS, stencilled on the side. These pop boxes, as they were commonly known, were used as seats for gossiping women. We knew the shop as Chissie's, although never in front of Mrs Chisholm. This frail and slightly stooping old lady, always served her customers in a slow and deliberate fashion. Why worry?, she had all the time in the world, and so did her customers, they weren't in a hurry to go anywhere, nowhere to go – this was a social gathering place.

The brass scoop from the scales was religiously brought round to the potato bag by Mrs Chisholm, intent on her task. Experience of years had taught her the feel of half a stone and she took a couple of odd small ones, to adjust the weight. The scoop was placed on the scales with a seven pound weight on the pan. She often used the principle of momentum to tip the balance, by dropping the last potato into the scoop, sending this with a click to the bottom. The scoop was whipped off sharpish and the load discharged into your basket before you could say, "Jack Robinson". My mam would sometimes say, "Bah, that doesn't look like half a stone to me. The old robber". But she always went back for more – it was so convenient.

There were certain women from our street who used to congregate in the shop, especially on Saturday nights, but not my mam. This was a good place to meet and catch up on the latest scandal and gossip. They sat on the pop crates or leaned on the counter and forwent their turns many times, just to smoke and gossip. This was before conversation killers, like television and bingo. This was real living. The scales seesawed and clicked all night long, with potatoes, sugar, flour, sweets and the rest. The gas light bobbed and hissed and the smoke from the Gold Flakes and the Craven 'A's ascended to the ceiling, like paternosters, amongst the chatter and the laughter.

You would never guess there was a war on. The little shop was open six days a week and closed late on a Saturday night. In those days, there were no shops open on Sundays. Nevertheless, if you went around to Mrs Chisholms back door on a Sunday morning, she would serve you, not that we ever did. It was unthinkable in our household that anyone should spend money and buy and sell on the Lord's Day. My mam would say, "It's a poor job if folks can't get what they need from the shops in six days, just laziness".

Now Golledges, in our street, were one of the families who never seemed to get themselves organised with provisions. They were always short of something for the Sunday dinner. Eileen, their eldest daughter, could be seen on Chissie's back step,any Sunday morning buying potatoes, peas or whatever, for their dinner. Mrs Chisholm drew the line at noon. There were limits, and after all she had her own dinner to see to.

CHAPTER 12

BULLIES

The school yard was only a stone's throw from our front door, although we were not allowed outside the gates during playtime. My mam would come to the railings and slip me a biscuit or two, ginger snaps, that she'd made, or perhaps an apple. These were soon greeded off me, as we would say, by the Town Head lads, who could smell any kind of food at a hundred yards. As soon as my mam's back was turned, they would descend upon me like bees around a jam sandwich. "Giz a bit Jos or giz thi gowk" from the local Mafia extortioner by the name of Harry Skint, as he muscled his malodorous body up to me. Gowk was local slang, for an apple core. I was pleased to just take a bite before parting with it to the hungry throng. There was bullying in our school, by the same crew. If you had anything worth taking, they would corner you in the toilets and tell you to turn your pockets out. If you didn't want a thumping you did as requested. Money, string, conkers or whatever, they took the lot. "Bring us an apple tomorrer an' don't forget or we'll get yer". This is how they survived in the jungle, dog eat dog, they lived wild and in filth. Being poor was no excuse, as my mam said, soap and water are cheap enough. They even had rival gangs that fought each other. Skint's gang and Blake's gang. There was a closed shop, boys were obliged to belong to one gang or the other, girls were not part of the gang culture, they couldn't fight. Boys who wouldn't join a gang were branded as cissies or lassie lads. Allegiance to one side or the other, changed like the wind, as pressures were brought to bear. Fortunately the bullying only took place during my early days at that school. Any boys caught fighting were thoroughly caned by the headmaster, which severely curtailed that activity. Discipline was imposed by the cane, you knew where you stood, there was no messing about. I had many a caning and it did me no harm, the deterrent effect was dramatic. Caning was to the hands, fingers to be precise and administered with vigour in front of the class. Some of the women teachers were not averse to the use of the cane and what is more, were respected for it. In our school there was a regular practice of a spontaneous slap across the ear with an open palm. This cuffing was perpetrated by male and female teachers alike and was worse than caning, made your head ring. None complained about this to their parents, most would have had another whack from their dad, for misbehaving at school. Girls were not usually caned or cuffed, they were made to stand in the corner of the room, facing the wall, until told to go back to their place.

I do however recall one girl in our class, who was about nine years old. Joan Gilkes was her name, always talking and disruptive. She was rather on the plump side, with curly ginger hair and had a foul temper to match. Miss Brown was our teacher and she could wield a mean cane, I can tell you!. Oh! what excitement on the day that Miss Brown reached the end of her tether. She dragged Joan screaming and shouting from her desk to the front of the class. "I'll teach you to scream at me," she shouted as she held the girl by the arm with one hand and gave her backside a good switching with her cane, as Joan danced and howled. She broke loose and ran out of the classroom, screaming, "Ar'm gonna tell me mam about you." She slammed the door shut and ran blaring away down the corridor, with a mouth like Shildon Tunnel. The headmaster must have heard the commotion, as he soon arrived at our classroom. He went into a huddle with Miss Brown, then left, looking worried. Our lesson continued and we were all on our best behaviour, awaiting the arrival of Mrs Gilkes. Sure as eggs were eggs, she would descend, like a harbinger of war, to unleash her wrath. The atmosphere was tense with anticipation.

We were not to be disappointed. Oh no! Miss Brown was reading us a story, when we heard the sound of raised voices down the corridor, where the headmaster's office was. She stopped reading. A high pitched voice, an angry woman's voice could be heard, getting louder as the footsteps came closer. The door flew open and in burst a large ginger woman with an angry red face , dragging a wet eyed Joan by the hand, with the headmaster in hot pursuit. Mr Siddle was protesting that she had no right to come in here and that he would fetch a policeman. Mrs Gilkes completely ignored him. "Is that her?". She boomed. Joan gave a nod. "Right, where's that stick?" She grabbed the cane from the table, took it in both hands and in one swift movement, she snapped it in half across her knee. "You touch her again and Ar'll break it across your bloody backside". Her anger was spent, the broken cane was hurled across the room at Miss Brown. The woman turned, grabbed Joan again, pushed past a bewildered headmaster and stormed away, down the school corridor. Joan's tears were replaced by a self satisfied smirk.

The atmosphere was electric, we had never experienced such high drama in our lives, the school bell was soon sounded and we ran to our homes for dinner, to re-tell the story, with excited laughter. The story was told, re-told, embellished and exaggerated no doubt, for many years after that event. Miss Brown was never seen in possession of her own cane after that, although she did borrow one from the next class when absolutely necessary.

Joan was not the only one with a temper. My sister's temper was sharp, when she was young. "She's got her paddy up", my mam would say. My folks couldn't afford to furnish the front room during the war, it was just used for storage. One day when Bette had got herself into a nice little paddy, she locked herself into the sitting room and did nothing but scream and kick the door. My mam was mad, couldn't get at her, she just shouted threats, "By jove, Ar'm goin' to take you through hands when Ar get hold of you,

you little toy", which made Bette even more defiant. The door was finally forced open and Bette got her desserts, a good spanking and off to bed, where she bawled herself to sleep. This remedy, acted like magic, she never did it again.

Not long after this trauma, Bette had a birthday coming up and mam said that she could have a party and invite some of her friends. She could ask eight only, as mam couldn't cater for more. Anyway Bette soon got her list, then wanted to add another. "Can Ar ask Evelyn Hall, please Mam"?, she implored, "oh please, just one more". The response was emphatic, "No!, eight is enough, anyway you hardly know Evelyn Hall". In an instant Bette's eyes flashed and she retorted, "If you were dead, Ar could ask as many of me friends as Ar liked". Deathly silence. Oh, what a scything blow. Mam visibly shocked. "And who'd bake and slave for the party then, if Ar wasn't here"?. Then she burst into floods of tears and went sobbing upstairs. Bette'd had her revenge, though not intended, I'm sure.

At school we were allocated free milk every morning, which we drank from a bottle. You queued for your milk at playtime. The milk monitor would punch a hole in the aluminium foil bottle cap with a pencil, stick in a straw and hand you the bottle as you filed into the hall. There was no question, of you not liking milk or you didn't want milk. Milk was good for you and a beady eyed teacher made sure that you finished the last drop of your one third pint bottle. The school lawns and flower beds were turned into vegetable gardens during the war, on a directive from the Minister of War. Our school was also supplied with a large wooden shed, which was built on the lawn. This was equipped with wooden cages, with wire netting doors, to keep rabbits. Rabbit breeding by the school, served the dual purpose of teaching us about the reproduction of animals and providing extra food for the nation. The work of looking after the rabbits, watering, feeding, cleaning out and so on was done by boys under the direction of one of the teachers. Those boys, who were classified as, thickheads, were assigned to rabbit duties, collecting dandelions, fetching hay and straw, cleaning out the droppings and so on. In the view of the staff, these boys were unteachable, so were put to good use with their hands. Prior to that, they had been assigned to digging the gardens and mowing the lawn, so this was at least more interesting. Boys would be sent to Brown's Sawmill, about a mile away to bring sawdust for the rabbit pens. I don't think I was thick headed, but nevertheless was once assigned to cleaning out rabbits and going for sawdust. However, I was called a fathead by Mr Siddle on several occasions. Going to the sawmill, was a great adventure for two boys, freedom to leave the school during lesson times and you could delay the trip, taking turns at wheeling the sack barrow and generally fooling around. We would spend a long time watching the large circular saw, slicing through tree trunks – waiting for sawdust, although there were mountains of it. The teacher gave us thre'pence to pay for the bag of sawdust. There were a number of doe rabbits that made nests in their cages and produced litters of baby rabbits. Then there were two buck rabbits, with a cage apiece. I think they were Flemish Giants, with big floppy ears. Nobody ever explained to us how the production line worked, they explained very little about anything at our school. You just learned what you picked up from the older sniggering boys, about the reproduction process. When the young rabbits reached a certain age, they were collected by a man with a big van and taken away. You can imagine that in those days of food rationing and shortages, that rabbits were much sought after. There were occasionally break-ins at the rabbit shed and rabbits would go missing.

This reminds me of another event concerning my mam, who made shopping trips into the town on a daily basis. She enjoyed going, 'down the street', which was the main street in Bishop. Her shopping was done in dribs and drabs, as she spread these enjoyable trips thinly, like margarine on a teacake, throughout the week. Outside of the normal school hours, it was a regular practice to take a short cut to town, through the school yard. In those times, the yard was locked, no-one was allowed into the school grounds, for whatever reason. We just climbed over the gates. One afternoon, my mam was returning home from shopping and decided to take the short cut through the school yard, during school hours. She must have been well

Hawker lads, dressing the horse with shamrock – St Patrick's Day

behind schedule to take such a bold decision. Half way through the yard, the headmaster's window was thrust open. "You aren't allowed in here", bellowed Mr Siddle, "rabbits have been stolen". She was absolutely speechless, dumbfounded, as she hurried on her way. She was in tears when she told my dad. "To think of me stealin' rabbits, what a great bully that man is". Nevertheless that was the end of shortcutting through the school for her. "Ar never want to meet that horrible man again", she blared.

My dad had firewatching duties, at one of the main electrical substations, in case of incendiary bomb attack. It was after the rabbits episode, that he was cutting through the school, late for firewatching. This was evening and dusk. He was confronted by the headmaster, wielding a torch. "This is private property", asserted Mr Siddle, but my dad was ready for him. "Get out of my way you little man, before I knock that unshaven head off your shoulders", he retorted, as he pushed him aside. The headmaster was not used to retaliation and was gobsmacked. How I wish that Norman Gornell could have seen him so treated, it would have been ample compensation for his boxed ear.

When Bette started school,I had to take her to the head-master's office, to register. There was no question of my mam going, not after the rabbits episode. Bette was terri-fied, so was I, as we stood by Mr Siddle's desk. "What's your name?" he barked. She was terrified and dumbstruck. "Bette", I whispered. "What's the matter, can't she speak", he snapped. A good start, I thought, and was pleased when that ordeal was over.

It was Palm Sunday, I shall never forget, we were going to chapel in the evening. Dressed in my new jacket and short trousers, I was all clean and spruced up. Now my friend Arnie, being a keen lad, had the idea of getting some palm leaves for St Peter's Church decorations. Everyone knew that palm trees didn't grow in County Durham, but weeping willow was a good substitute, after all, it was the thought that mattered. I was just hanging around outside our house, waiting to go to chapel, when Arnie appeared up the street, brandishing a large butcher's knife. "Hey Jossie, give us a hand to get some palms over the tower, Ar've bor-rowed this gullie off our Billy". No sooner said than done, we were up over the water tower wall in a jiffy. There was a massive tree, bearing pussy willows. "Wi man, this is just the job" said Arnie, "you grab a hold of this branch and bend it ower". He wielded his gullie like a machette. "Oh! sorry Jossie", as we both looked at the gash in my left little finger which had been cut to the bone. I never could stand the sight of blood, made me feel faint. Quickly I scrambled over the wall into our back street, scuffing my new shoes in the process and managed to get into the house before pass-ing out like a light. My dad applied iodine and bound up the wound. Needless to say, I missed chapel that Palm Sunday and often think of the episode when I look at the scar.

Our teacher in the top class was Mr Bull. He would teach us to sing patriotic songs, usually with Miss Bruce at the piano. We would assemble in the hall, where we would stand in rows. A favourite I recall, was 'What shall I do for England, that's done so much for me?' The girls sang dutifully, but us lads would mutter amongst ourselves. "Done for me? England's done nowt for me", and snigger. "Sing up you boys and stop grunting", Mr Bull would snap. Another song, we knew as, 'Marching through Georgia.' We had never heard of 'The Battle Hymn of the Republic', or at least it had never sunk in, as they say. He never explained what the song was all about, which would have made it more interesting. When we got to the bit, "So we sang our chorus from Atlanta to the sea", well, we knew instinctively that this should be 'Atlantic'. Mr Bull would stop us abruptly at this point with a loud roar. "Atlantic, Atlantic, how can you march from Atlantic to the sea. That is the sea!" We were perplexed. Oh for a map, a simple explanation and any child would understand. However, he wasn't aware of the impact of visual aids, only the impact of the bellowing voice and the clipped lug. Despite the tuition, we always sang Atlantic, we just knew that we were right.

Patriotism was instilled into us during the latter years at Etherley Lane School. We knew that to be English was something to be proud of, we were a superior race, conquerors of the world and rulers of the British Empire. We were given the clear impression that other nations, foreigners, were inferior. There was no suggestion of learning a foreign language. "Let them foreigners learn English," was the attitude.

It was at that time, that the BBC, was starting broadcasting to schools. This was novel and enjoyable, at last we were being exposed to good effective teaching methods.

For the broadcast, 'Singing Together', our class would assemble in the hall and sit in rows on the floor, legs crossed. The school wireless was switched on and we would wait for the announcement. "Good morning schools" and then we would be taught to sing simple songs, with rapturous music, never heard by me before. I marvelled at the beautiful melodies, played on a piano. Little did I know, but this was my first exposure to classical music, particularly of Mozart and Schumann. The words were often from a nursery rhyme. We would listen and then sing, as we imagined that thousands of other schools would be doing likewise.

> *Pussy cat mole*
> *Jumped over the coal*
> *And in her petticoat*
> *Burned a big hole*

We sang to a beautiful tune, only recently discovered to be 'Sonate' by Mozart. Us lads would snigger amongst ourselves as we substituted some of the words and often wondered how many of the countless throng of singers did the same, throughout the land.

> *Pussy cat mole*
> *Jumped over my hole*
> *And in her petticoat*
> *Burned a big mole*

Oh we were adept at anal humour, if little else. What merriment this caused.

At playtimes we would often play Cowboys and Indians on horseback. Being a big lad, I was always a willing horse. The object was to charge about with your mount, whilst he tried to dismount another by grabbing and pushing. Tommy White was a smallish lad and used any form of persuasion to get his way. "Oh howi Jos, giz a bullet or Ar'll not let yer be me hoss". What a cheek, I was the best horse around.

CHAPTER 13

GROWING OUT

My mam made her own curtains for the windows and covers for the chairs, she would, run them up, as she termed it, on the 'machine', never, 'sewing machine'. This was a Singer, which had been given to her by someone. It had a foot operated treadle that she rocked up and down with her foot. There was a big wheel, driving a round leather belt up onto the machine, with its shuttles and bobbins of thread. She would let me work the treadle, when she was loading the little shuttle reels. This was done on a small attachment driven by a rubber wheel, which you swung onto the handwheel. I was fascinated by this machine. There was time late in the war when there was a craze of making your own butter from milk. We had a Kilner jar, with a glass lid and a rubber seal, these were usually used for preserving fruit. Anyway my mam would pour the cream off the top of the milk bottles and put it in the Kilner jar. She would sit shaking it, then my dad would offer, "Ar'll shake it a bit if yer like Vi". We all had a go, new fangled as we saw a lump of butter forming out of the cream. It seemed to take ages, but helped the butter ration. I had the idea of fixing the jar to the treadle of the machine with string to give a rocking motion. "By what brains", my mam found it easier to sit working the treadle to make butter. She could do this as she prodded the mat, doubling production. It's as well that the Ludites never got wind of this or our machine may have been smashed with sledgehammers, to save the jobs of the buttershakers! What frivolity, but there was a germ of inventiveness emerging in my young mind.

The headmaster announced one day at school, that children whose feet were growing quickly, could have them measured and would be issued with extra clothing coupons, depending on age and foot size. This only applied to boys as I recall. Those of us who thought our feet were large for our age, had to line up in the headmaster's office to have our sizes checked on a measuring device. For some obscure reason, we had to give the name and occupation of our father. "What's your father's job" questioned the headmaster. "He's a jointer, sir", I replied. "You mean joiner," he bawled, as he wrote it down. Who was I to argue? Several of us qualified and went home clutching clothing coupons for our mams. There were two items of footwear that were always in short supply, these were wellingtons and black plimsolls, that we always knew as sandshoes. The news would spread through the town like wildfire, Doggarts have got sandshoes in. Mams could be seen hurrying there, before they were 'soled' out. People who lived a bus ride out of Bishop, stood no chance in the sandshoe rush.

My dad had a shoe repair last, on which he used to sole and heel our boots and shoes. This was a three legged cast iron affair, with a large foot, a small foot and a heel. He would usually do his cobbling on the floor in front of the kitchen fire, with the clipping mat rolled back. He used a sharp, cobblers knife to cut the shape from a leather sheet, after he'd marked round the shoe with a pencil. The soles were then left to soak in a dish of water until they were supple. When the sole had been tacked and hammered into position, it was smoothed round with a file and then finished off around the edges with a kind of black sealing wax, applied from a stick and a hot iron smoothing tool. Very smart shoes were produced, usually with rows of steel studs or protectors to make them wear longer. Good for sliding on the ice. Real leather was a rarity during the war years and therefore my dad was very pleased to buy some synthetic leather from Woolworths. This was a marvellous

Bishop Market Place – 1935

material, it looked and smelled of real leather. As his shoes were in need of repair, he thought he would sole and heel these using this leather substitute and very smart they looked too. I recall it was winter time, the snow was melting and slushy under foot. He'd been preaching in some remote country village. When he came home he exclaimed, "Look at what the slush has done to that Woolworths' leather", as he lifted a leg. The smart new soles and heels had been transformed into a tattered mess, of what looked like soggy cardboard. With that, we all had a good laugh.

As I mentioned earlier, my dad believed in friendly societies, and we belonged to the Foresters and the Rechabites. I used to take the Foresters money to Mrs Milner in Durham street and get our card signed. Often I was sent to pay the Rechabites. I thought it was some kind of disease, related to rickets and dog bites. Nobody explained what it was all about. The Rechabite woman was severe and harsh with me as she took my card and my sixpence and made me stand just inside her door. "Stop that sniffing boy", she would snap, "you want to blow your nose". I was, a great sniffer, keep it in, not blow it out, that was my philosophy on the common cold. Her husband had a stiff leg, always laid up on a sofa, with a stick by his side. To my boyish mind, this had something to do with a dog bite or the rickets.

Sometimes there were rows between my mam and dad, part of married life I suppose. She would go off the deep end and 'played war with him', a lovely Durham expression. She would get to feel unappreciated by the rest of the family and had a rather harsh way of bringing us down to earth, when she was being taken for granted. She once told Bette and me that she was sick and tired of us and threatened to leave, but we never took this seriously.

Until one day, we returned from school. We came to the front door as usual, it was locked, we knocked and knocked, but no response. The back gate was locked, we hammered on it to no avail. Unusual we thought, mam was always there. No problem for me, up I climbed on the gate, foot on the sneck and scrambled over the wall and dropped down onto the dustbin. The gate was soon open and Bette came in. We were not latchkey children, we had no key to get into the house. I soon got on the roof of the scullery, and up to the landing window, which was of fancy glass, with some small red panes. This was locked, so there was no way in. Dejected, we just sat on the back step by the bin, wondering if she'd left us. She'd said she would, "go away and never come back". Perhaps her threat had come to fruition. We just sat there and felt very close to each other. I felt protective to our Bette. We were relieved when she appeared, after what seemed a long time.She said she'd had to go down the street. I must admit that we became more appreciative for a while, after that shock to our systems.

CHAPTER 14

OLD MAIDS

A pair of the most fascinating characters in our street were the Miss Winskills. These were two maiden sisters, who lived next but one to us. Their names were Mary and Sarah and when we first moved into the street, they would both be well into their eighties. They lived their lives in the past, in the reign of Queen Victoria. They dressed Victorian, they thought Victorian, they breathed and lived as though Queen Victoria was still on the throne, with The British Empire intact. When they went to town to do their shopping, they always linked arms. They wore long dark coats and buttoned boots, their pot pie hats, were pulled well down over their ears. Mary was almost deaf, whereas Sarah was nearly blind, they needed each other, they functioned as a pair, like Siamese twins. I learned later, that they had lived in a small village, just across the River Wear, from Bishop Auckland and had been brought up there with a very strict father, who forbade them ever to have any young men callers. They were sheltered in their upbringing and when their parents passed away, they moved to our street and continued to live their lives as recluses, cut off from the modern world, living in the past. They took no newspaper, had no wireless, no electricity, only gas lights on the wall in their kitchen and sitting room. The Miss Winskills had no relatives, no visitors ever crossed their threshold.

These old maids were self sufficient, they obtained all of their requirements for life, in their weekly shopping trip into the town. I suppose they must have had a pension to sustain them. The people in our street were friendly and neighbourly, typical of Durham working class families. The Winskills however were withdrawn from the world. They lived in their own world and shunned any outside intrusions, however well meant these may have been. This existence worked for many years, when they both had reasonably good health. A severe and long winter, I recall it well, changed all that. My dad was very kind to people, especially old folks and would clear the snow from their front pavements as well as our own. He was never to ask, just did it.

My mam would offer to get them provisions at the shops, when the conditions were too bad for them to get out. She would fetch their bottles of medicine from the doctor's surgery. They were very grateful and mannerly, but she was never invited in. They got to know us as neighbours who could always be depended upon to help them out, if there was anything they needed. My mam had gained their respect. She would say to me , when I came in from school, "Would yer go along to Winskills, they want yer to go to the doctors to collect their medicine".

As a boy I was a bit scared of them, they were an odd couple. Sarah would park herself on a stool behind their front door. She would sit there for hours, peeping into the street through the letter box, which she propped open with a matchbox. There she would sit, looking into the outside world. Liked to know what was going on, without being involved. It was unnerving as I passed that door. If the letterbox was open, I knew she was watching. There was a step up into their house, which made the letterbox level with my eyes, as I passed by. Her eyes were glazed and watery with the draught – she wore no specs. Although I didn't want to, I was somehow compelled to turn my head. Our eyes would meet, whereupon I would immediately break into a gallop, towards home.

They must have been very tough to withstand the cold, as their only means of heating was the black kitchen range, where they kept a coal fire going. Anyway the Miss Winskills got to know me through my parents and would give mam the empty medicine bottle to take to Doctor Wardle's dispensary, to be re-filled.

The lady at the doctor's dispensary knew exactly what was required and I soon came back with the full bottle. I would feebly knock on their front door, hoping that there would be no one in, but knowing that there would be. In a little while there were some fumbling noises from within and the bolt was drawn, the latch was lifted and the door slowly opened. Round would peep Miss Winskill's face, mop capped as always, her hand shielding the light from her eyes. "Is that Brian. Have you got the medicine?" I handed it over. She would offer me a penny, from her pinnie pocket for doing the errand. However, I protested, "It's alright, no thanks". But she was insistent. Her hand was held out, not flat but bending back, a dirty grubby hand with cracks and sores. In the middle of her palm would be a penny, always an old one, Victorian.

My mam told me I shouldn't accept anything for fetching the medicine, but Miss Winskill insisted. "Thanks very much," I blurted and darted back home. "Oh mam, what awful hands she has, all dirty and sore". "Ar'll give that penny a wash in case you catch something", said mam, as she ran it under the tap. "You'd better come and wash your hands, before you get your tea".

When dad came in from work, we related the tale to him. "Eeh, poor old dears" he would say "nobody cares for them but us, Ar'll just pop along after tea to see if they're alright". He was always received with courtesy and good manners, but never invited into their home. That is before the snow storm and big freeze up, that winter.

My mam had called, with some bits of shopping. Mary and Sarah both came to the front door. They must have been desperate. "Mrs Joslin, do you think Mr Joslin could have a look at our lavatory, it's frozen up, and the yard's blocked with snow"? "Wi yes, we've had the same trouble, it'll be no bother. When Fred comes in from work, he'll pop along and see what he can do," my mam offered.

It was a cold night, my dad had walked from work, no buses, no good for bikes, no bike anyway. "Come on Brian,

Ar'll need your help, get the shovels out of the coal house."
He disappeared down the cellar to get the Tilley lamp, a
blowlamp, and some paraffin.

Tilley lamp lit, wellied and gloved, off we went and
knocked on the Winskills' front door. "Come in Mr Joslin.
Bah, what awful weather, we're all frozen up". Oh, what an
adventure for a small boy. Sarah holding a candle, led us
along their passage to the kitchen and opened the door.
The gas light was burning, the fire was almost out and
there sat Mary on a chaise longue, wrapped up and trying
to keep warm. "It's Mr Joslin and Brian, Mary. Mr Joslin's
going to mend the lavatory", she shouted. The room was
dingy and dark apart from the bobbing gas mantle on the
wall bracket. Wallpaper from the Victorian era was peeling, doors and cupboards were dark brown. The floor was of
stone flags with dirty clipping mats. There was candle
grease everywhere. Because of Sarah's poor sight, she felt
her way around, and there were dirty greasy patterns
along the wall to the fireplace, where she had felt her way,
over the years. "Me sister doesn't hear very well you know
Mr Joslin", said Sarah. "Oh that's alright honey, Ar'll just
have to shout". "What's he say Sarah?" – "What's he say
Sarah?" This was Mary's constant cry. "Mr Joslin says he'll
shout Mary, so you can hear," she repeated into her sister's
ear.

I was so enthralled with these goings on, I didn't notice
the smell at first. There was the smell of the candles, the
smell of the gas, the smell of the coal fire, a stale smell, but
the lavatory was across the yard. "Anyway honey, we'll just
go and clear a way across the yard first. Now you stop in
here and keep yourselves warm". shouted my dad. "Come
on Brian, we'll take the Tilley lamp and shovels."

We entered the scullery, which had a candle burning on
a shelf. Now Winskills' scullery, unlike ours was equipped
with a stone sink under the tap, with a plug hole to run the
water away. An up-market version of our house, you might
say. The stone sink was brim full of liquid, the drain obviously frozen solid. The stench was suffocating, I tried to
hold my breath. The Tilley lamp revealed all, what a mess.
I felt sick. "Ar think we'll concentrate on the lavatory first,
bah, let me get that door open". The back door was soon

opened. The snow, what with that off the roof, was three feet deep and solid. Dad started digging and soon cleared a space on the window ledge for a Tilley lamp. A good shoveller my dad was and he soon started making headway towards the lavatory.

It was now snowing again, but good to be outside. The large flakes hissed as they settled on the hot Tilley lamp where they instantly turned into steam. "Eeh, have you ever seen such a sight Brian, it's a wonder they've not got consumption". He gradually cut a channel through the packed snow, and I piled it high to the side, against the yard wall. It took ages to get to the lavatory door and free it open. There was no smell here, everything was deep frozen. The pan was brim full and solid. "Right now, Ar'll just get the blow lamp goin' and leave it in here with the door shut". No sooner said than done, paraffin rags alight, the blow lamp was soon lit, pumped up into action. It was soon roaring with a hot blue flame with the refreshingly clean smell of paraffin.

He then cleared a way to the coalhouse and we took some buckets of coal into the house. Dad soon had a good fire going. "Don't worry honey", he shouted, "everything'll be alright, Ar'll be back later when it's thawed out". With that we left and it was soon my bedtime. I don't know how dad sorted things out. But he did. The Miss Winskills were very grateful. "Eeh what a kind man", they said. "Now listen to me honey, Mrs Joslin will bring you some nice home made broth, to keep out the cold". I think my mam and dad saved their lives on that bitter winter's night.

My parents had a genuine love for people in unfortunate circumstances. They put their faith into action. Reward enough, to see a job well done and to lend a helping hand.

So that was the start of a neighbourly friendship with these two old maids. After that, my mam would go along and see to them, do their bits of washing, ply them with her rejuvenating broth and teacakes. Neither of them were very well, after that bitter winter and my mam would often sit with them. They wanted all the news off her, which she would relate. Mary would continually interject, "What's she say Sarah, eh! what's she say". Then Sarah would repeat in her ear. So it went on. As my mam sat there, she would often see a mouse venture out from somewhere and creep along the hearth, looking for bits of bread and crumbs that Sarah was in the habit of dropping whilst making toast. The making of toast had to be seen to be believed. Poor old dear, she would cut a thick slice of bread, then impale this on a toasting fork, her eyesight was not too good, much worse than her sister's. She would hold this to the red fire until it smoked. There was soot, there was coal dust, there was toasted bread, mixed together, good clean muck, as they used to say. The smoking charge, was deposited on the bread board, then dunked with a dollop of butter from a knife – more by feeling, than by seeing. This was placed on a plate, "Here's your toast Mary". The mice thrived as you can imagine.

My mam would see the sisters to their bed, a four poster with a big patchwork quilt. I saw it. A candle was required to ascend the stairs. The wall of the staircase was shiny with years of groping and sliding. The stair treads at each side were thick with years of candle wax. The thin, threadbare runner up the centre had escaped most of the wax. There was no gas upstairs, so the candle had to suffice. Tough old birds, what! If they'd had the pampering of modern old folk, they would have outlived Methuselah.

They had a collection of Victorian magazines from their younger days. One day Sarah asked my mam if she would like to borrow some of these magazines, they showed the latest fashions. "There's a section on, THINGS FOR BOYS TO MAKE," she said. "Your Brian can learn how to make a kite, but don't let him see this one, it explains how to make a catapult." Little did she know that I already had a catapult and what is more, it was well seasoned with use! There was many a broken bottle and broken window to prove it.

Kites were always homemade then. They were based on a cross of canes or wooden laths, framed around with string which was pulled tight into notches. This skeleton was then covered with brown paper or newspaper which was folded over and glued together with a paste of flour and water. The real skill, which was learned by experience was in fixing the string, anchored at two points. For the tail, newspaper strips were rolled into tight bows and

Victorian Schooldays

secured in a row along a string. You had to wait until the next day for the paste to dry, before you tried out your new kite. The wait was well worth it. With the right wind, it would soar as high as the clouds, so it seemed and was the source of hours of fun for girls and boys alike, not to mention dads.

As my little sister Bette, was born during the war, she never knew anything but sweet rationing. Sweets to her were like opium to an addict. Now these old maids had a large jar of boiled sweets, just like those in the shops, which stood on the sideboard. Where or when they acquired this jar of sweets, I don't know. "It must have been before the war!", my mam remarked. I wondered, which war? The jar looked so old, you couldn't read the label. It was about a quarter full. These sweets were unwrapped of course, as sweets were then. The hands of the Miss Winskills must have dived in there many times over the years. Bette couldn't wait to go along there with mam. "Would Bessie like a sweet?" they would question my mam, as though Bette couldn't answer for herself. They always called her Bessie. Bette Davis meant nothing to them, but they had heard of Lilian Gish. Bette's eyes lit up, this was the highlight of her visit. In went Sarah's hand, out came a sweet. "There you are pet," Bette loved it, and became immune to a whole catalogue of diseases, suffered by other children of her age.

Sarah had been a good seamstress and dressmaker in her younger days and liked to feel Bette's dress, as she could hardly see. She would tell how they were always taught to remove all buttons before washing a garment. This was done by carefully unpicking and removing the thread, to be re-used. Such was their thrift, learned by necessity, by living through hard times.

As a family we got to know the old maids much better because of that harsh winter, but they were to remain virtual recluses for the rest of their lives.

CHAPTER 15

KIT AND CONKERS

As there were no telephones in working class homes, various other means of communication had to be used. Word of mouth, handwritten notes, knocking on the fire back with a poker. The human mind is very inventive and resulted in most bizarre action concerning Mrs Kell, who lived almost opposite,across our front street. My mam was ironing one evening in the kitchen. Suddenly there was a thump on the front door. Then another thump. She thought it was lads throwing stones, as they often did, so went to investigate. It was a winter's evening and foggy outside, when she opened the door. I ought to explain here that in wartime, one of the cheaper foods was meat paste, which came in small tins. These were rationed of course, like all food, but some people had hoarded a good stock before rationing started. There were several of these tins on the pavement and in the gutter,outside our front door. A voice shouted through the mist from opposite. "Bah!, yer must be deaf in your house, howay here, and get me the doctor, Ar'm poorly". Mrs Kell was found to be lying with her front door open, in their passage. "What a sight, my mam said. She'd fallen and crawled to the door in her nightgown and mop cap, looking pitiful and pasty faced. I doubt if Mrs Kell had received any training in the throwing of hand grenades, but two out of six was a pretty good score in my reckoning. Needless to say, my mam got her coat and went along to Doctor Wardle's house for help.

Now these were an odd couple, I always thought of them as being old folks, they were probably in their late fifties. Mr Kell was named Kit, he always wore a cap and walked in a peculiar plodding fashion. With his characteristic walk, his footsteps were unmistakable as he came up the street. My dad said that he had, 'dead feet'. The heel touched down first, then his sole followed with a flap, like a flat fish dropped onto the fishmonger's slab. F-lap, f-lap, f-lap, f-lap, always at a slow and deliberate pace, coming up the pavement like a troglodite in hot pursuit of a tortoise. Kit, like my dad, worked for the Electricity Supply Company. He was a general labourer and in fact, my dad was influential in getting him set on in the firm, when he was out of work. He said that he regretted this, because Kit wouldn't work, he was above digging trenches. Painting, replacing dud lamps and other light duties were allocated to him. Besides this, he felt that he was a cut above the other labourers, wore a suit for work and he, 'knew everything'. Self opinionated, he enjoyed starting arguments, seemed to thrive on conflict like some people do.

His wife, so it was widely believed, did everything for him. She put his socks and boots on, fastened up his laces. She fastened his tie and fetched and carried all meals. He did absolutely nothing, why should he, he had a perfectly good servant.

I recall shortly after the tinned paste episode, Mrs Kell was taken seriously ill and passed away. Of course my mam being a softie, offered to do his cleaning as she felt sorry for him and his predicament. Not only did she clean, she fetched his groceries and often gave him a bowl of her nice vegetable broth for his supper. "There's some nice hot broth, "she would say, "it'll warm you up". On Sundays she always took his dinner over, roast beef and yorkshire pudding. He paid her one pound a week for this service, more money for my mam to squander! She would get his rations, his cigarettes, groceries, sweets and general provisions. One day she had collected his sweet ration, all in Wrigleys chewing gum, he preferred this to any other sweets. She took his shopping over, so that he would have it when he got back from work. On this particular occasion, Bette was with her and helped to carry the shopping across, to put on his kitchen table. Anyway as I previously mentioned, our Bette had a sweet tooth and she took a packet of chewing gum, the temptation was too much. Besides, one packet out of eight would never be missed. My mam did a recount before she left and found that there was a packet missing. She confronted Bette who was by this time playing in the street with her friend Maureen.

"Bette, have you taken some of Mr Kell's chewing gum?" "No"! "Come here, let me see, open your mouth." Sure enough there it was. Maureen had also been given a piece. My mam went off the deep end, she played war with her and sent her home to bed. Chisholm's shop was still open, so the shortage was replenished from our rations. Kit never knew anything of this.

It was some time later that my mam learned from another neighbour that Kit had been having a moan. "Ar'm sick and tired of that ard broth she brings me, it's always the same". What an ungrateful man. She was furious – that was the end of doing for Kit, she gave in her notice straight away.

He wasn't pleased, as you can imagine – began to stew. A few days later, my dad was working in Shildon on a fault and his jointer's tent was pitched on the pavement as usual. Kit was in his gang that day and he'd never spoken to my dad since my mam ditched him. He was outside, tending the coke brazier and my dad was sitting on a tool-box, just inside the tent, preparing a lead sleeve for the joint. Kit must have been simmering with anger. Suddenly he took a dive at my dad, got him by the throat and pushed him over the toolbox into the side of the tent. My dad was totally shocked and perplexed by this spontaneous attack. Kit had to be hauled off by Jack Shaw, his ganger and another man. "What's that for," exclaimed Jack. "He knows" retorted Kit, as he was dragged away shaking his fists, "he's the one man Ar'd like to murder." My dad didn't retaliate, that was not his way, which left Kit rather flat.

It was some months later that Kit found a lady friend

Dad and Jack – taking a breather

who lived in a nearby village. He sold his house in Lindsay Street and moved in with her. However, nothing was straightforward with him. The lady in question had a daughter. Enough said, Kit got to fancy her more than her mother. When the mother found out, you might understand, the fat was in the fire. There was an almighty shindig and he was put out of their house. He then took lodgings at the Wear Valley Hotel in Bishop. Soon he was at loggerheads with the landlord, so was obliged to leave. He was an awkward old so and so and no doubt moved on to vex somebody else. The one thing that I did gain whilst my mam was looking after him, was a portable wireless set. This was a massive affair and needed a dry battery and accumulator to power it. It was of no use to him, he didn't use it, too mean to buy batteries. I said to my mam, "d'yer think Mr Kell would sell us that old wireless?", hoping that he would give me it, after all she'd done for him. He offered it for two pounds. I had some money saved and agreed to buy it. Oh what joy, my own wireless, I could take it to our allotment and listen to my favourite programmes. I knew I was robbed, but got great pleasure out of that set. I took the accumulator to a man in Etherley Lane to be charged. He had a big battery charger in his garage, and provided this service for the people in the vicinity. Re-charging cost fourpence. People with battery sets, usually had two accumulators, one on the set and a spare one, kept charged.

There was an old lady who lived next to Kell's house. Mrs Dobson, was always known as, Old Ma Dobson. She always wore a long skirt and a pinafore, hair tied back in a bun. Now she was a widow and must have been in her seventies. She would often ask us boys to run errands for her to the shop. I shall never forget the day we were snowballing in the street. Old Ma Dobson came to her door. She called me and asked me to go down to the shop for some potatoes. Now this was unlike me, but I must have been having such a whale of a time, running about in my wellies and my balaclava to keep my ears warm. "It won't take a minute", she said. I ignored her and carried on with my game. "Brian, come here," she said, her voice now raised, as she beckoned me. Once within arms' reach, she clicked hold of me by my balaclava, hauled me towards her and smacked me across the ear with her spare hand. She was a strong woman, even if she was getting on a bit. My head rang like a church bell. When I brought her potatoes back I knew never to ignore her again or anyone else for that matter. Another useful lesson had been learned in the University of Life.

Sometimes my mam's brother, uncle John and aunty Jenny would visit us from Houghton. This was always a time to look forward to. My dad was no sportsman, but uncle John would play cricket with me, show me how to hold the bat and how to bowl with a spin. Once when they came, it was the conker season and we all went for a walk in the Bishop's Park, where there were lots of horse chestnut trees, bearing ripe conkers. During the annual conker craze that swept the town, lads would head for the park.

Uncle John – my 'Conkering Hero'

By throwing sticks up at the conkers, you could bring down showers to collect. As you can imagine, the lower branches were soon denuded, leaving the really choice specimens out of reach. Uncle John had strong muscular arms because of his job as a coal hewer down the pit. It was no trouble to him to throw a stick to the highest branches and bring down showers of choice conkers. I came back absolutely laden, with plenty for my mates.

Who would be conker champion this season? All sorts of concoctions were made to develop a really hard conker. Some lads would soak them in vinegar, then dry them in the oven, in attempts to toughen and harden. The hole for the string was made with a meat skewer or a small screwdriver, before the hardening process. Some claimed to have secret recipes for toughening, using meths or paraffin. Last year's conkers were banned, illegal, as the real hardener was time. Anyway we had great fun with conkers, spending many an hour taking turns to try to smash each other's out of existence and increase our score.

One day I was playing conkers with a lad called Alan Patterson, who lived with his grandmother, near to Carl. I swung my conker with such vigour that I split his in two. One piece went straight through a window pane into their front room. As you would expect, his gran was very annoyed. But when I told my dad, he soon measured up for a new sheet of glass and replaced the pane. It was an accident, not deliberate and no harm done.

CHAPTER 16

SNOW AND MUCK

My dad made me a new sledge out of an old bacon box from the store. This sledge was squat and strong with iron clad wooden runners. Mr Neasham, the local blacksmith, had made him the iron runners to fit, out of flat iron bars, which were fixed in place by countersunk screws. Two holes were bored through the wood at the front by means of a red hot poker, to take the pulling rope of old sash cord. For extra comfort he covered the top of the sledge with a piece of coco-matting, tacked into position. A new sledge was not much use until it had been broken in with use, when the naturally dull and rusty iron runners would become shining and polished like mirrors. This little sledge could achieve phenomenal speeds or so it seemed and gave me many many hours of pleasure and thrills, which were second to none in my young life. Beginners would sit on their sledge with feet sticking forward and wellies raised from the ground, to be used for steering and braking. The position favoured by us lads was lying flat on your tummy, known as a, 'belly flapper'. Both hands forward gripping the front of the sledge and legs spreadeagled like a swallow in flight.

The typically clad sledger in the 1940's, wore two pairs of knitted woollen stockings, with wellingtons. Short trousers were always worn, as this was the conventional dress, until breeching at about the age of twelve. It was unthinkable to wear your dad's old trousers cut down, you would never live it down and would be branded a cissie by other lads. Long trousers were not available in boys' sizes, that was not the fashion. If you were lucky, your mam had knitted you a balaclava helmet to keep your ears warm and maybe a scarf tied around the neck. We seldom wore knitted woollen gloves as these were of little use when they became soaking wet, which they soon did. Girls were similarly clad except that they wore skirts instead of trousers and a pixie hat. Novices served their apprenticeships on the lower slopes of the rec. However we soon became highly experienced and skilled and sought more challenging sledge runs in the foothills of the Himalayas, where we could become daring and adventurous.

Clarence bank was to us the Anapurna of Bishop, its mighty slopes, its glaciers, its avalanches. Rumour had it, that there were Yetis also, inhabiting the snow caves. This bank was one of the steepest around, not only was it steep it had a bend about half way down. With skill you could negotiate the bend and head for Nelson Street at the bottom, which adjoined and began to level out. Lots of bairns would sledge on these slopes for many hours in freezing conditions, oblivious to discomfort or the passage of time.

A favourite sledge game was cops and robbers. You gave the robber about two counts start. Then, sledge clasped to your chest, you would run, then dive head first onto the slope in hot pursuit. The objective was to dislodge the robber from his sledge, often as not coming off your own, to continue rolling down the hill, clasped together like a snowball. We would arrive home, exhausted, with glowing faces, numb fingers and knees. My mam would apply Snowfire ointment to my sore legs, mainly knees and the red-raw ring around my wellie tops. By the following day you were again fit for active service.

There was a rumour that we were to have a new teacher in our school, for the class next to the top. This must have been announced in morning assembly. She was a lady teacher, Miss Haddie was her name. She could speak French, so we were told, although we were not taught any foreign language in our school. We were so ignorant of any foreign languages, but must have had some inkling of French. Why? Well, because we had learned that the French said, "we-we" for yes, that was enough motive to learn that translation, although we knew not the spelling. It soon got around in the school playground that we would have some fun with Miss Haddie. A joke was born. Some bright spark suggested, "Ar'll say, please Miss can I go to the lavatory? She'll say, we-we. Then Ar'll say, no! pa pa." This flash of wit, caused great jocularity and howls of boyish laughter. The joke was told and retold, till it was spent, no longer funny.

And so, in the fullness of time, Miss Haddie arrived as our new teacher. She was petite, blonde hair and very with it! She soon learned to control the unruly element, send them to the commandant, the headmaster. He knew how to deal with such disruptive boys. He had, 'Ways'!

So we learned not to mess about with Miss Haddie. Sure enough she taught us some French words. The pen – la plume, the window – la fenétre, that's all I remember of her French lesson. She was a maiden lady, couldn't cope with sex, swearing, horsemuck or any such degrading subjects. The nearest we got to animal reproduction was when I brought some frog spawn to school at her request. This was Nature Study or 'Naturesterry', one word as we heard it pronounced and believed to be correct.

My life to that age of about nine years old was kept in very low key, mainly by my mother. We were working class, we were inferior to the upper class, we could not aspire to anything very much in life. In fact we were second grade citizens, keep low, head down, don't try to crawl out of the gutter, that's where the likes of us belong. This was what was instilled into us, if not in so many words. I had volunteered to bring some frog spawn to school but never expected or wanted any publicity. I was therefore taken aback when Miss Haddie wrote on the blackboard during Nature Study, something for us to copy into our books.

LIFE OF THE FROG
6th May Brian Joslin brought frog spawn in a jam jar.
13th May Black dots getting bigger.

And so on, to be added to each week, as we observed the progress of the developing tadpoles. We never knew and we were never taught anything about spawning and fertilisation. Oh no!, that would be getting too close to nature.

When my name was put on the blackboard, I was so embarrassed to see it there. My name, a nobody, on the blackboard, it might as well have been up in lights in the market place. I was pleased when the tadpoles were finally hatched and returned to their pond and the words were finally rubbed out.

Then the horsemuck episode. There was a family by the name of O'Kelly, who lived at the top house in Clarence Street at the other end of the school from us. We, as lads would often pass their house, on our way home from being down Bishop. Now the O'Kellys had two girls and two boys, they didn't attend our school, they were Catholics. Enough said, we were at loggerheads, the hatred was mutual. Patrick was about our age, a cheeky faced boy, arrogant, calling us names. This didn't go down well with us lads. They would shout names at us, insults to our ears and then they would run and dive for cover into their front porch and passage. Oh, how foolish of them to think that they could retreat to a safe haven.

It was Saturday morning, there was Stoney, Howard and myself. We'd been down to Pallisters to collect some pies for my mam and were wending our way home up Clarence Bank, minding our own business.

About half way up the bank, the O'Kelly boys appeared, hurling abuse. "Yeller bellies, yeller bellies, can't catch us". "Right" I said "let's learn them buggers a lesson, we'll hoy some o' this hossmuck at them." As usual there had been horses on the bank and they had left us a plentiful supply of ammunition. The horsemuck was firm, round and fresh, like khaki snowballs. We gathered our ammo and chased our tormentors to their house. As usual they screamed insults as they ran to their haven. Not so safe a haven now! We were on their heels and let them have a few volleys. We hurled our deadly ammunition, as they dived towards their porch and we didn't hold back! With replenished supplies, we bombarded them, their porch, their hallway, their stairs, with horsemuck. We went running on our way, rejoicing in our victory. The day was ours without a doubt. We compared accounts with each other as we ran home laughing. "Ar giv that Trevor one right in the lug," I laughed. "That's nowt," bragged Stoney, "Ar hit Mick right in the gob," as we hared away, euphoric in our victory.

Oh woe!, oh woe! The day of reckoning was yet to come. Mrs O'Kelly, when she returned home, was not amused, she of course heard one side of the story, but the evidence was there. First thing Monday morning, off she went to see our headmaster to relate the sad tale. "Those boys are nothing but dirty ruffians" she told him, "they should be well punished, I know their names. It was premeditated, they even came prepared with a bag of manure. They're a bad lot, this disgusting attack was planned." Sure enough after playtime we were summoned to the commandant's office. We couldn't deny that we had bombarded the

The Store Baker – a supplier of ammunition

O'Kellys, and yes, some horsemuck has gone into their house. To say that we had pork pies in the carrier bag, only made things worse. We were obviously lying. Without more ado Mr Siddle lined us up. "Hands out," he barked as he reached for his cane. He gave each of us six of the best. With stinging fingers and throbbing hands, thrust under arms for ease, we filed back into our classroom.

Miss Haddie singled me out, to explain. The other two boys went to their places. "Well, what's this all about Joslin, why have you been caned"? I stood like a dummy, unable to open my mouth. "Come on tell me", as she pushed me by the shoulder, nearly knocking me over. She was smaller than me, but fearsome. How could I mention the word horsemuck to her, it was like swearing. "Please Miss we chased some boys and threw things at them" I stammered. "Threw things, threw things!" she screamed, "threw what? Tell me!" After some hesitation – "Lumps of manure," I volunteered. There was a gasp and then stunned silence. "Oh you animals, you're disgusting", she had turned as red as a beetroot, with embarassment, as she smacked me around the ears. "Back to your seat you horrible boy," she shouted. We resumed normal school life once again. Poor Miss Haddie. We had no more trouble with the O'Kellys after that episode, they had been suit-ably subdued, it had been well worth the caning.

The next incident involved Mrs O'Kelly and muck, not horsemuck this time. It was several months after that saga. There would be three or four of us lads, wearing roller skates. They were all the rage in that summer. As we came back from the rec, up the bank, I had a tremendous urge to empty my bowels. As lads, we never made a big issue of this, if we were in the fields or rec any convenient dyke or trench would suffice. If not, there were always back lanes for emergency use. Because of our recent history with that family, I didn't dare to knock on their door to ask to use their lavatory, besides there wasn't time.

I shot around the back lane, O'Kelly's back lane and found a place by the water tower wall. There was no-one about, I dropped my trousers and found instant relief. A quick wipe with a dock leaf and my trousers were almost up again. At that instant there was the click of a sneck.

Mrs O'Kelly appeared at their back gate. Oh, what a surprise, she knew me on sight. "What do you think you are doing, oh!-oh!" she cried,"what a disgusting trick." I was away, following my pals down the back lane, trousers half mast, roller skates and all, what an embarrassment. She would be too disgusted to go to the school again and dreaded the knock on our front door. This came soon enough and my dad answered. They talked for a while, then he came in. That Mrs O'Kelly says that you did your business on her back step. "Ar couldn't hold it dad, honestly, it happened in their back lane, but not on their back step". "Now, after tea, you come with me and we'll go round there, you must say you are sorry to Mrs O'Kelly." Off we trundled, my dad and me, it was only two streets away, five minutes walk. I was so shy and embarrassed, didn't know how to face the situation.

Sure enough the evidence was there, a neat little pile. "Is that it"? asked my dad. I nodded. "On the back step, on the back step, it's many a mile off the back step," as he paced it from their gate. "Wi, that's twelve yards", he said as he knocked on the gate. She appeared, wearing a scowl. "Brian's come to apologise. Go on, say you're sorry". "Sorry Mrs O'Kelly, Ar couldn't wait, Ar'll never do it again." "You could have used our toilet if you'd only knocked on the door, there was no need for that". She didn't understand, there was no use in explaining, I was too embarrassed to explain, even if I could have done. My dad came in, "Mind you Mrs. O'Kelly, you said it was on your back step, it's twelve yards off, Ar've just paced it out". "Back step was a figure of speech" she explained. That was beyond my comprehension. She seemed satisfied at that and closed the gate. My dad removed the evidence in a brown paper bag that he had brought with him and off we went back home. This affair was kept from the school. I dread to think how I would have explained my predicament to Miss Haddie. My dad often told this tale, when we had company at home, to make them laugh. He got them rolling in the aisles.

CHAPTER 17

GOLLY

One of my best friends during the war years was Arnold Golledge known to his mates as Arnie or Golly. The Golledges were a large family and lived in No 13, about halfway down the street on our side. Mrs Golledge was petite, and very smart as I recall, always wore high heeled shoes when she went out, invariably sporting a cigarette. Arnie's dad was a soldier and a prisoner of war in Germany for most of the war. I never saw him until the war was almost over when he returned. He was an athletic man, an amateur boxer and kept himself very fit. Now the Golledges had four girls and three boys of which Arnie was the youngest. They had a dog and two or three cats. A rough and ready sort of family, but not dirty in any way. Their table in the kitchen for meals was bare wood and scrubbed, at each side they had a matching wooden bench, one against the wall. By this means they all managed to get seated. When they had finished their meal, plates were handed down to Gyp the dog, who greedily licked them clean, before they were washed in the sink. Anyway, Gyp was a clean dog, almost one of the family. They had only two bedrooms of course, but managed alright. The eldest son Mark was away in the Navy on convoys, which made more space. Poor Joan was taken away to the fever hospi-

tal, when she was about twelve years old. "Oh that's the
fever ambulance", the wives in the street would exclaim.
What kind of fever it was we never knew, but she died in
that hospital. All the family wore black armbands, an old
tradition for a period of mourning which lasted two weeks.

Billy would be in his teens when I knew him, worked at
the butcher's shop at the bottom of our street, learning the
butchering trade. He was a tough guy, an earlier version of
Marlon Brando. He taught us how to make a good catapult,
to shoot starlings and spuggies, bottles off a wall, or anything else you fancied. This was wartime and some of the
components were difficult to come by. The 'Y' piece or
wooden stridlers as we knew them, could easily be
obtained from a hawthorne dyke. It took a keen eye to spot
a good pair of stridlers in the hedge. Thongs of leather to
anchor the rubbers to, and to make the pouch were cut
from the tongues of old boots or shoes. Sometimes leather
ends of old braces came in useful. The rubber was difficult
to come by, but we knew of an old car in Stevenson's field,
just through the hedge of the rec, behind the trenches. This
car had been abandoned, just conked out I think, with no
parts to be had. We would slip through a gap in the hedge
with our sharp jacknives. The tyre wall was strong and
took a bit of cutting through. Once through you could get
hold of the red rubber inner tube and pull sufficient out to
get some nice strips, about half an inch wide and nine inches long. Billy was keen to help me, as my dad was the
source of some good insulating tape, 'Bulldog Brand', he
used it in his job. There was always some in our cellar. My
Dad would often enquire, "Where's that Bulldog, Ar'm sure
Ar had some Bulldog in my toolbox." He would fetch some
more. "Ar'll lock up that toolbox. Brian's always got my
tools out all over the place, Ar'll get a lock on it," he would
moan to my mam. Although he threatened on many occasions, he never did lock it up. Our cellar was also the
source of copper wire for binding the rubbers onto the
leather thongs. We all became crack shots with our catapults. Billy would shoot birds, but I never could do it. I preferred bottles which we scavenged from dustbins. We
would line these up on the water tower wall and blast
away at them with pebbles.

There was broken glass everywhere, we would get chased away for making such a mess and then go to the Dam Head, where we would shoot pebbles to our hearts content at bottles thrown into the river or at insulators on the telegraph poles. The Dam Head was not far from us on the river Wear, pronounced as in 'weird', without the 'd'. The river had been dammed across so that the water could be channelled off to the waterworks nearby, for purification into drinking water. This was then pumped up to the water tower, at the highest part of the town, at the top of our street. This was only a small dam, no hydro electric scheme, but there were salmon boxes to allow the fish to travel from the sea at Sunderland, to their spawning grounds in the upper reaches of Weardale.

Just upstream from the dam, was a stretch of river with a sweeping bend in it, the Dam Head. There were deep parts for swimming and diving and shallow parts where you could wade across with your shoes and socks off. About a mile further upstream, was the village of Escomb with its famous seventh century Saxon church. There were the ruins of a Roman camp, Vinovium, about five miles down-stream, at a place called Binchester. The Saxons had removed stones from the abandoned camp and ferried them up-river to their settlement at Escomb. These were used to build their little church. Some Roman engraving could still be seen on the stonework at the side of the church. One of the stones, was clearly marked, Sixth Legion, (LEG V1), but upside down. This was thought to signify the over-throw of the Romans, by Christianity.

The Dam Head was our great adventure playground, where we could cross the river looking for birds' nests, we all collected birds eggs then. A popular hobby that cost you nothing. My mam didn't care for me going to the Dam Head, it was dangerous in parts and occasionally there was someone drowned there in the deep part, known as, Twenty One Foot, also a favourite place for suicides. The river often burst its banks, especially when the snow melt-ed in the spring. There were large marshy pond areas, with frogs and newts. Further sport for our catapults. Billy was older than us, and fearless, he would climb the highest tree for birds' eggs. His trick was to carry the eggs in his mouth, so they wouldn't break, this left his arms free for climbing. I'll never forget the time he slipped and fell on his way down a tree. He bumped his face on a stump and this caused a large swelling, which closed his left eye. He just picked himself up, grinned, opened his mouth and produced two wood pigeon's eggs, unbroken. His face was like a boxer's, who had taken a good punching. Tough as old boots he was, never winced or complained, a true Brit, our hero. Although there was a school at the top of our street, for some reason, the Golledges went to another school at Cockton Hill about two miles away, which they walked to. Everybody walked to school then, including the teachers.

Pocket money was hard to come by, but we often picked up a few coppers, literally. I recall when we were lads, we would gather around the wedding crowd, outside of St Peter's Church, or St Anne's Church, any church for that matter. It was customary, that when the newly-weds emerged from the church, the gates of the churchyard would be only opened, by gift of money. However this was not the case in Bishop. When the happy pair appeared, then the groom or the best man would reach into his pocket for money to throw. If this was not done immediately, then a group of scruffy lads, and that included me, would start to chant. "Shabby Weddins, Shabby Weddins, Shabby Weddins", and so on. The groom would then reach into his pocket and throw handfuls of coppers into the air towards us. When I hear that song, "Pennies From Heaven", I recall those showers of pennies, ha'pennies and farthings that we scrambled for, amongst the feet of the wedding guests. Inevitably, there were urchins from the Town Head, like highly skilled terriers in pursuit of a barrel of rats. But Arnie was sharper than any of them, and usually ended up the richest.

Then there were the telephone boxes, as they were always called, dotted sparsely about the town. People had to put tuppence in the slot, to reach the operator, who would then get their call. There were two buttons on the cash box, marked 'A' and 'B'. "Putting you through. Please press 'Button A' " or "Please press 'Button B', and try later". Whereupon their two pennies would return with a tinkling sound into a receptacle. Us lads never made phone calls, for one thing we had better things to do with our money and what is more, we knew nobody with a telephone. Wouldn't know what to say anyway. Whether by poor design or absent minded, carelessly rich people, the cash box would often yield a few coppers. You just pressed 'Button B', which started a ticking noise, then bunched the underside of the cash box with your boot. If you were lucky, then it would pay out, just like a 'Win All' machine at the showground.

CHAPTER 18

STEALING

Near the bottom of our street on the opposite side, just above the butcher's shop there was a back lane, that led to the butcher's yard and then turned and ran up behind the houses. This was not a paved back lane like ours, but just earth and cinders, which was unusual. A close boarded high fence, separated it from the allotments, where people grew vegetables. Some had greenhouses with tomatoes and flowers, others kept hens. Immediately over the fence running the whole length of the backway, was a row of Victoria plum trees, with some of their branches hanging over the fence. You can imagine the temptation as the plums ripened. Being wartime, fruit of any kind was hard to come by, as were sweets. This made the plums irresistible. Very few became fully ripened, they were sought after by everyone who knew of their whereabouts. I suppose the allotment holders were the righful owners of those trees. The occupants of the houses down that back lane, also laid claim to the plums. We, the local lads thought they were fair game, to be plundered, as we plundered any fruit trees in the area that we knew of. These poor old trees took some stick, during those war years and after, it's a wonder they ever survived to blossom and bear fruit each year. They were climbed, they were shaken, and their branches knocked with clothes props to dislodge the fruit. We were always being chased from those trees, as we wouldn't let the plums ripen. If they even became yellow, then we knew they would be picked or knocked off to save them from us. What a predicament, we would bite them, green and bitter, then spit them out, they gave us belly-ache, but that never deterred us. The very high ones would escape to reach maturity, but even some of those were shot off with our catapults, damaged and bruised. Stones would go astray and hit a greenhouse, we would hear the crash then scarper, until the coast was clear. We would fire stones into the air over the allotments to break the glass of cold frames or greenhouses and we did this for fun, just for the thrill of the noise of breaking glass. When I grew older I regretted this sort of damage that I had inflicted on good honest folks, pursuing their hobby, working hard to produce foodstuff. Many is the time that I wish I could undo that damage, no-one ever pinned it on us. I wish they had. The majority of those plums, ripened in darkened drawers until they were fit to make jam. There were other plum

Folks grew their own tomatoes

trees, apple trees, pear trees, in private gardens behind high walls. Nevertheless these would be raided.

One of the crazes we had, was playing darts. Not with a dartboard as you may expect, but into a boarded fence, around behind the butchers shop. Someone would chalk a large face on a litte body, with eyes, nose, mouth etc. Usually, of Hitler with a moustache, fat Mussolini or slit eyed Tojo. Numbers were chalked onto the various parts of their anatomy for scoring, there was no rudeness as you may imagine. We had our standards and never hit below the belt. Darts were not easy to come by, but we managed to acquire one apiece and had great satisfaction in throwing these at the enemy leaders. Our darts were of heavy brass, with a steel point that was kept sharp by honing on a stone step. The wooden shank, screwed into the brass part and divided into four to take the flight which was made from folded paper. There was one lad, who had moved to Bishop from Liverpool, by the name of George Harris. I thought he looked more like George Formby, with his buck teeth. George would hang around our gang, always begging for a go with our darts, which we were never keen to relinquish. He would say, "Oh, come on, let us have a go, we've been bombed out. Our house is gone. Oh, come on please, you don't know what it's like to be bombed out". Eventually, he wore us down, we took pity on him and let him join us. I used to wonder what I would do, if we were bombed out of our house and felt so sorry for his plight. Poor George, boys are cruel, we would poke fun at his accent, which was different from the way that we spoke.

Sergeant Dexter lived in the next street, Ladysmith. He was a special constable, a fierce and stern man, who would often scold us for lighting bonfires or committing other minor misdemeanours. He had a walled garden with some nice apple and pear trees, at the top of his street, flanked by the water tower wall. As lads, we were often over the water tower, which was surrounded by a high stone wall. Once over the wall we were on Water Board private land and could easily hide behind that wall out of sight. It was fairly easy to drop over the wall into Sergeant Dexter's garden.

Stealing

One Saturday afternoon, Arnie and me spied these beautiful ripe apples, too good to miss. Over we went, there was no-one about. Scrambling up an apple tree apiece, we filled our pockets. We always wore short trousers, and one of my pockets was completely torn open, which led to the lining. Very handy for carrying apples. We almost had as many as we could carry when the gate opened with a click. There stood Sergeant Dexter. We were caught red handed. Like startled deer, we bolted, dropping apples as we went. "I know you boys," he shouted, "I'll be round to see your parents." We were soon over the wall, quickly unloading our pockets into the long grass. "We'll shig these out later", gasped Arnie. Then, down our back lane we went and across the road towards the Dam Head, our happy hunting ground and safe haven. Arnie would be alright, his dad was away and if Sergeant Dexter went to his house, he would get plenty of lip from his mother or elder sister. He wouldn't waste his time going there.

With me it would be different, I would be in real trouble. It started to get dark soon. The evil hour could be put off no longer. We made our way back towards home. I said, "So long" to Arnie, "see yer tomorrer". I heard my name resounding down the street. My mam was at our front door, calling for me, as mams did then. She just stood at the door and hollered my name "Brian, Brian", as loud as she could. She spotted me coming slinking up the street. "Where've you been, Ar've been calling for you for the past hour, you've got me worried to death". "Ar've just been down the Dam with Arnie", I admitted. "Down the dam, the dam, yer know Ar don't like you goin' down there, it's dangerous. Look at them clarts on your shoes." She clashed me round the ears as I ducked in. "Get in that house, you little monkey, Sergeant Dexter's been round here about you, you little thief.

"Ar've told you about stealin' apples. You'll finish up in Durham Jail if you go on like this." I was sent to bed in disgrace. Our Bette was already in bed. "Have you got any apples left Brian" she ventured, hopefully. "Ar've hidden'd some over the tower, you can have one tomorrer." I couldn't imagine what my dad would say, he would be so disappointed in me, and tomorrow was Sunday.

CHAPTER 19

CHAPEL

My dad had been out somewhere during the saga of the apple pinching and for some reason was never told about the episode. Perhaps my mam was too ashamed to admit that her little Brian was a thief. He must have been late home that Saturday night.

However late he was, he never forgot to make the jelly for Sunday breakfast. Now this may sound a bit odd, but my dad always made sure that we had some nice jelly for Sunday breakfast. There was method in this ritual jelly making. He always took Bette and me to Wesley chapel, to the morning service. There was always a children's story. But children were allowed to leave before the sermon. My mam never went to the morning service, she was too busy making the Sunday dinner.

You can imagine, as youngsters we were not keen to get up and go to chapel, but we were expected to and had to go! There was no question of us not going. To make things easier for us to get up, dad would shout up the stairs at nine o'clock, "Come on you two, yer jelly's out". The very thought pulled us out of bed like a magnet and downstairs we would rush, Bette in her nightie and me in my pyjamas. We always got dressed downstairs, by the fire. How we loved that jelly, strawberry, lemon, raspberry, whatever the flavour, it always went down well with bread and butter.

We got washed and dressed in our Sunday clothes, the nightclothes went into the cupboard next to the fireplace where they were always kept warm. Off we would go with dad, down the street, along Etherley Lane and down Princes Street to Wesley chapel, the one with the clocks.

We were late without exception. I never recall being early, in all the years that we attended the morning service at Wesley, as we always knew it. As we entered the vestibule, the first hymn was in full flight. We were handed hymn books by the steward. "Hello Fred, lovely morning, hello pet, hello pet. There's your hymn books. They've just started Fred, second verse". In we would march, to the second row from the front. Most people sat towards the back rows of the church. My dad detested this, being a preacher and having to shout to the back, so he tried to set an example for people to move forward. We would file into our pew below the pulpit, sit and bow our heads, as we were always taught to do when we went into chapel. Then if there was a verse left, up we would stand and join in the hymn. If it was the last verse we would remain seated for the prayer which always followed the first hymn. Often as not we would arrive too late to go in during the first hymn and would have to wait, whilst the prayer was offered. Then, the congregation joined in the Lord's Prayer. The second hymn was announced, then we would go to our seats. I think our clock should have been 15 minutes fast instead of 10, this would have solved our problem. But I'm thinking like my mam now!

Sunday was a day of rest and a day of worship in our family. In the afternoon Bette and me would go to Sunday School and then sometimes, but not always, we would go to the evening service, especially if there was Holy Communion, in which my mam liked to participate. Holy Communion seemed to mean more to her than all the sermons anyone ever preached, perhaps this was her Anglican upbringing.

I must have been about three, when I started Sunday School at Wesley. Although I remember little about the early days in the infants' department, I do recall the main Sunday School, which I attended for many years. Sunday

School was held in the afternoon, in the schoolroom, adjoining the chapel. There were lots of children in attendance at that time, and even the most unlikely and seemingly unreligious families placed importance on sending their bairns to Sunday School. The superintendent was Mr Scott, who owned the fish shop. He was a kindly man, with a beaming smile and wavy hair brushed back, like my dad's. He conducted the proceedings from a desk at the front, below the stage. There were rows of dark brown cane chairs, and wooden forms down the sides of the hall. Each class would occupy a row of seats, with its teacher at the end, next to the aisle.

We would sing children's hymns and be lead in prayer by Mr Scott. We always had an offering and you usually were given a penny by your mam to put in the collection, which was taken up on round wooden plates, lined with red felt. After the money was blessed by Mr Scott, the plates were taken away for counting by Mr Hutchinson, who was the Treasurer. I got myself into a panic one day when, by mistake I put a half crown of my own money, that I'd saved, into the collection. Mr Hutchinson must have thought he was doing well, when counting up the proceeds, nobody ever gave that much. I timidly explained my mistake. "Ar've put me half crown into the collection instead of this", as I offered him the penny. He just laughed, "Yes, I thought you'd made a mistake Brian" and he returned my half crown in exchange for the penny. What a relief that was. Then, we would assemble into our own classes, in groups around the room to listen to stories from the scriptures, or later to read in turn from Bible passages. The teachers over the years must have been very patient and kind, as some children were a bit disruptive. At the end of the Sunday School year, we would have the Sunday School Anniversary, usually in the summer. This was held in the Chapel and a great deal of work was put into the preparations by the teachers. We rehearsed songs and hymns to be sung and many children learned recitations, to be given during the services, usually afternoon and evening. All of the mams and dads would come to chapel, often the only time they did attend, to proudly watch their bairns perform.

Although I learned recitations, I was so painfully shy and was petrified by the thought of having to stand up and recite in front of a congregation. I would beg my mam and dad to excuse me this ordeal and they must have understood, as I was never made to perform, although our Bette did. She was very nervous as most children were and although I had listened to her rehearsing at home many times, I would be in a cold sweat until it was all over for her. Then I felt a sense of relief and a glow of pride for my sister, for she had done something that was beyond my capabilities.

Always on my return from Sunday School, we would call at aunty Millie's house. This was not our real aunty, but a friend of my mam's, Mrs Wright. She would always give us an apple each and a threepenny piece,for which we had to say, "Thank you very much aunty Millie", before we ran off home. We were never allowed to spend our money on Sunday, although some of our friends did. We were taught that Sunday was the Lord's day and was special. There were plenty of other days in the week to buy things. We would never have thought of disobeying, we would have felt so guilty and knew that God was always watching us.

When we got home from Sunday School, our first job was to change out of our best clothes. My dad always taught me to hang my Sunday clothes on a hanger, straight away. "You'll always keep them smart and clean for going to chapel".

In the summer evenings after chapel, we would often go for a walk along by the station and then up the black path to Latherbrush Bridge. I would sport my own walking stick, a junior replica of my dad's. One thing I couldn't resist, was slashing nettles with my stick. This would annoy my dad. "Now listen here, Ar'll take that stick off you, if you don't stop that," he would threaten. It was no good, I was, and still am, a compulsive nettle slasher!.

Two of our Sunday School teachers, were the Curry sisters. They were also professional school teachers, at Witton Park village School. Their names were Maude and Mildred. Maude, must have seen a spark of potential in me, when it came to entering for the Scripture Examinations, which followed a course of study. I would be about nine years old, when she took me aside one day, into the vestry. "Come in here a minute Brian, I want to talk to you about the Scripture Examinations". The thought of examinations petrified me, I was no good at school. What's the point, I thought. Anyway, she explained that she would be teaching me with three others and this would be in the vestry, every Sunday morning, during the service. Her sister Mildred was to coach another group of four. Anything was better than sitting through a boring service and I agreed to have a go. I must say, my dad was very pleased that I had agreed to take this step. The course started and I soon got interested in the subject, and discovered that Miss Curry had a way of making the bible stories come to life. She gave me a lot of encouragement, as she coaxed me along through the course. I'd never in my life experienced this high standard of teaching and soon began to respond. I even worked on my own at home, in preparation for the weekly progress tests.

After several months of work, the examination day finally arrived. I was a little nervous, detested exams, was never up to them. The papers were handed out to us, as we sat around the large table in the vestry, with our Minister invigilating. This was the first examination in my life that I actually enjoyed, as I tackled the questions, one after another. When the results were issued I turned out to be top of the group with 96 per cent. My dad was very pleased and remarked, "You know Brian, one day you may be a preacher like me". This made me feel very happy, to receive such praise from him, my efforts had been really worthwhile.

Sometimes we would go with my dad to one of the country villages where he'd been to preach. We would occasionally be invited to spend the day with one of the chapel stewards and his family. I would be about ten years old, when we were invited to Cockfield. This was quite a large mining village, just beyond Lands. The day of our visit was a very warm and sunny Saturday. We went to the home of Mr and Mrs Kirby, who lived at the bottom end of the village, opposite St Mary's Church, the Methodist chapel was higher up the village. We got off the O.K. bus and just had to cross the road. There was Mr Kirby waiting to greet us. "Hello Fred," said Percy, as he shook my dad's hand. "Hello Mrs Joslin, nice to see you again, come on in. Our two are waiting to meet your bairns and Annie's just makin' a pot of tea." We followed him in, through the porch and then into the kitchen. Mrs Kirby was just coming out of the pantry, where she had been attending to the foodstuff for tea. She wore a great big smile and a lovely clean pinnie. The introductions were made, amongst lots of laughter. Their two bairns were there. Audrey was about my age and Neville a bit younger. I thought that Audrey, was a 'real smasher', with her lovely smile and long dark hair, which she wore tied back. Neville was a lively lad, very clean and smart, no doubt spruced up for the occasion by his mam.

He said, "Ar'll just go and tell mother they've arrived." Strange, I thought, his mother was here! I soon learned that his mam's mother, Mrs Coates, who lived next door, was always called 'Mother', by all the family. She soon appeared, another beaming face, then more introductions and laughter. My dad was always at his best in company, he liked to make people laugh.

The grown-ups all settled down to cups of tea, with biscuits. Meanwhile, Audrey and Neville, took us outside to play. We went into mother's yard, just round the corner, where there was a garden with lovely flowers and some outbuildings. As I have said before, I was very shy, painfully shy. And very withdrawn, partly due to my nature and partly to the way that I was brought up.

Conversation didn't come easy to me, I felt awkward and inadequate. Bette was not shy and only about five years old at the time, she was in her element, as they say. She soon wanted to go to the toilet, what with all the excitement and everything. There was an earth closet in mother's yard, just like at Lands and Sedgefield. Audrey said, "We sometimes play shops, Brian, would you like to play. Being shy I just said, "Yes". I was dumbfounded. She soon got things organised, with an old table for a counter and some bits and pieces from the house. "Now I'll be the shopkeeper," she said, "and stand behind the counter." Neville, Bette and me were the customers. I recall little of the events that followed, but one thing sticks in my mind. Audrey was cutting up an apple into small pieces. These were 'sweets' and would soon be wrapped up in little packets made from newspaper. Playing shops was something new to me, I'd never done that before, it was so exciting. This was mak-believe. It seemed real to me. Playing shops with Audrey, was indelibly etched on my memory and I recall little else of the other games we played. I never imagined in my wildest dreams that one day, she would be my wife. Didn't even imagine that I would ever get married, "Who would want me?", I thought.

In our street, there was a hawker-cum-gypsy family who occupied the house next to the butchers, separated by a back lane. The house was peculiar in some ways, different from the rest in the street. It had a large back yard and a stable for one horse. This was the Mounsey family. Mrs Mounsey was a neat and tidy lady, gypsy stock, black hair, silk headscarf, golden ear-rings, gaudy dresses. Everything in their kitchen was polished and shining, the black range, the brass fender, the ornaments, the horse brasses. She was spotlessly clean and very houseproud. Mr Mounsey, better known as Lather, was her husband. What a charac-ter was Lather, so named, I believe, because of his dislike of lather, that is soap, as a lad. Or it may have been his love of soap, who knows. I always knew him as a clean man – perhaps Mrs Mounsey cleaned him up.

Lather would often get his horse and cart out from his yard and go on his rounds, to earn a living, selling fruit, kippers, herring, or whatever commodity was seasonal. His nephews were Jumbo, a big lad and his brother, Scranner. 'Scran', is a hawker name for bread. A good eater is, a 'good scranner'. In our family we pick up words and use them whatever the source. I always call bread, Scran, even to this day. "Fetch a loaf of scran out of the freezer".

Jumbo would often come up our street with his horse and flat cart, just called, 'his flat'. This is how words are born, how new words evolve. He shouted as he peddled his wares. "Taties, taties. Tatie buyers, tatie buyers. "Calling out the wives to buy his wares. So, by me, to this day, potatoes are referred to as, 'Buyers'. Singular – 'Buyer'. A word is born. "Ar think Ar'll just roast meself a nice buyer, for me supper. Delicious with a bit of butter on it".

Audrey was 'a real smasher'

When I knew Lather during the war years, I always thought of him as an oldish man, much older than my dad. I would often pass him on the lane, as he walked along to the Maid of Erin for a drink, or when he staggered back, the worse for wear. A kindly man, "Hello bonnie lad" he would shout out to me as I passed him. Gone were the days when he would fight any takers in the bar, so we heard. A good fighter in his younger days, but now he had calmed down a bit, perhaps the gypsy's spell. They had a son, John, a tall lad, as I recall, with long dark greasy hair, he would be about the same age as Billy Golledge. Bunnie was his nickname because he kept rabbits. He also bred prize bantams. Billy used to say, "Bunnie has a big black cock, you should see it, it's won prizes." Bunnie was famous for his big black cock, more than that I don't remember of him. Hawkers had their own words, with origins in their Romany roots. For instance, hawker men would greet each other, "Now charver!" different to pitmen, who would say, "Alright marrer?", or "What fettle?"

'Caller Herrin' was the cry

My sister and me fancied keeping rabbits in our back yard and pestered mam and dad until they agreed to the idea. My dad managed to get some old wood boards and soon made a nice rabbit hutch, with a felted roof. We bought two young rabbits from a lad at school. Mine was a grey rabbit with a white tail, Bessy Bobtail. Bette's rabbit was a different breed, black with white patches. Inevitably this one was christened, Peter Whiteleg. At that time, the staple diet of pet rabbits, was dandelion leaves, known locally as 'rabbit meat'.

We were so thrilled to have our own rabbits, especially in the early days and would rush home from school to see them. Out we would go to collect rabbit meat. Alas we were soon tired of our new life with pet rabbits, when it came to cleaning out the hutch and going to the sawmill for sawdust and getting straw for bedding. I think we had them about a year when my dad reached the end of his tether. My mam said to him when he came in from work, "Ar think those two are gettin' tired of them rabbits, there's no rabbit meat for them. Would you see if you can find a bit in the back lane, before your tea". He soon gave us an ultimatum, "Now look here, you can't have pets if you don't look after them, they'll have to go." There was a man at work who would have them and give them a good home. We didn't take a lot of persuading and so they went.

CHAPTER 20

BUMPS IN THE NIGHT

Before Golledges moved into Number 13, there had been a man living there by the name of Willie Atherton. He'd committed suicide, by gassing himself. That's all we knew. Children have vivid imaginations and the Golledges were no exception. When the younger ones were in bed, lying quietly, almost asleep, the bedroom door would slowly open. A hand would appear round the edge of the door. This was the hand of Willie Atherton, the previous occupant, coming to get them. It was an older sister or brother playing a practical joke. Then, they would say that they had seen the same thing – a wizened hand. There was always the unmistakable smell of coal gas. Then of course I would relate the tale to my sister, when we were in bed, to frighten the life out of her, so that she would put her head under the sheets. But she loved it, the excitement. Although she was frightened, Bette always wanted me to tell her more ghost stories.

We slept together in our young days, in a large bed in the back bedroom. There was a light in the middle of the ceiling, with a bowl like a dish, hung on three chains. This bowl had swirling patterns on it, that sometimes looked like faces, especially when you stared at it. We would always implore mam, "Please leave the light on mam, we're frightened", but we liked to be frightened. When I told Bette a creepy story, she would shriek and scream. If Mam heard, she would come steaming up the stairs in anger. We could hear her heavy footsteps ascending quickly, to scold us, but at the same time, were relieved when she appeared. She dispelled the ghosts immediately. "What have Ar told you Brian, frightening our Bette like that, now get to sleep. Ar'll put the light out". "Oh mam no! leave it on please, please," we would plead. She would leave it on, before going back downstairs. "Tell me about the old woman in the churchyard, Brian". "There's a hand coming round the door", I would answer, "it's Willie Atherton". Then she would bury her head under the covers to stifle her shrieks.

The morning was a new day, all the shadows and ghosts evaporated in the sunlight. There was a time when we were obsessed by the idea of ghosts. A gang of us lads would get properly dressed up, to go ghost hunting. Old raincoats over our shoulders, fastened with a single button round the neck, like a cape, each with a stout stick, we ventured around the local back streets, during the dark evenings. Dusk was the best time for ghost hunting. Once someone thought they had seen a character known as, 'Sandshoe Pete'. We never knew if he was real or imaginary, but we hunted him down to an empty house, not far from us. This house had been empty for a long time and had a spooky atmosphere surrounding it. We climbed over the back wall and into the back yard. There were some stone steps leading down to a door, a cellar. It was locked, but we could hear a rustling and a dripping sound. We were sure that Sandshoe Pete was in there. If he'd appeared, we would have died of fright.

Charlie Emery may have sometimes been mistaken for the elusive Pete, as he always wore sandshoes, as he shuffled along. He was a well known character then and we were terrified of him. There was something not quite right about Charlie. He had one twisted leg and a shuffling gait, dragging his leg. Head twisted to one side, with one shoulder raised above a limp arm. His speech was undecipherable, he spoke with a grunting voice. He could run very fast though, and snored loudly as he ran. It was widely rumoured that he liked to look at girls' knickers, so became known as, Mucky Charlie.

I think he was a bit fond too, and would become very angry and annoyed when we yelled at him. "Mucky Charlie, Mucky Charlie," and would set off to chase us. We only did it to get chased, what a thrill. Lasses would tease him from the school yard, where they were safe. If they spied him going by in the rec they would chant, "Mucky Charlie – can't catch us". "Ar'm not mucky", he would snort angrily, what a shame, I think he was quite harmless.

The part of Bishop where we lived was in 'Pollard's Lands', so named after a young peasant boy, who had lived in the seventeenth century. According to folklore, this boy was given these lands, as a reward by the Bishop of Durham, for ridding the countryside of a wild boar, which had been terrorising the area. We had an allotment just next to the Pollards Inn, a local watering hole. Before the war, Howard's dad had been there occasionally, for a pint, swore that they watered the beer down. Howard once chalked on the pub door – Durham County Water Board, what a sense of humour. My dad was teetotal, so never frequented this pub, although water would have done him no harm. He would have drowned before he was drunk.

Our allotment was always known as, 'The Garden', as we had no garden adjoining the house. There was a workmate of dad's by the name of George Hopwood, who also had a garden there and he helped him to build a wooden shed to keep his implements and plant pots in. The shed was made from secondhand creosoted boarding and consequently always had this very strong, not unpleasant aroma, especially when the sun was on it. The roof was covered in black felting, fixed in place with large headed galvanised felting tacks, to keep it watertight. There was a window with overlapping panes of glass, like in a greenhouse. The hinged door had a turnbutton to keep it shut and a hasp and staple for the padlock. If it came on to rain whilst we were working in the garden, then we could shelter in our shed, until it stopped. I imagined that camping would be something like this, with the sound of rain pattering on the roof, a cosy feeling, very exciting.

Dad sent me for water, "Go and fetch another can of water Brian". Off I would go, to the one and only tap, in the

Our creosoted shelter from the rain, in the garden

allotments, near Mr Hopwood's garden, to fill our watering can. Some people had greenhouses and collected the rain-water from the roofs in a water butt. Mr Hopwood had an old galvanised poss-tub where he mixed sheep droppings, with water. "That's good an' rich Fred" he would say to my dad, "just help yerself when yer like, it's grand for cabbage plants."

Poor Mr Hopwood, his little boy had died at the age of five, he'd been a bit older than me. I'll never forget the day when he called me over. "Howay with me pet, Ar've got something for yer". He took me into his potting shed which ajoined his greenhouse. Reaching up into the top of the rafters, he took down a small garden fork with the tines wrapped in sacking. This he carefully unwrapped and handed it to me. "This used to be our Billy's fork Brian, when he helped me in the garden. You can have it, so you can help your dad to dig your garden". I was thrilled to bits. "Look dad, Mr Hopwood's given me this fork, it was their Billy's". "Eh, isn't that champion," admired my dad, "now you'll have to look after it, and keep it clean. You can hang it in the shed next to mine". He gave me a little plot in the garden, so that I could grow cabbages, caulis, shallots and lettuce. These, I tended with care, until they were ready for picking. Then I would hawk them, around the doors, to neighbours, with our wheelbarrow. My dad had made this from an oblong wooden box, with two shafts to push it and a pair of old pram wheels on an axle.

When I was younger he would let me ride in the barrow, as he pushed it empty to the garden – coming back it was usually laden with produce. Anyway I did well with my selling vegetables. I was very shy, but even so, would knock on doors offering cabbages for threepence and lettuce for tuppence. Some people thought they were too expensive and wouldn't buy.

Once, when I had sold my last cabbage in Clarence Street, I ran pushing the empty barrow, excitedly towards home, with my newly earned pocket money. In my excitement and haste, I'd tipped the barrow, too far forward, so that the front touched the whizzing ground. Over I went into a heap on top of the upturned barrow with wheels spinning. I limped home, pushing it, smarting from my scraped knees and hands, wondering if it had all been worthwhile, to earn two and fourpence. My mam soon washed my wounds and dabbed on iodine, which was kept for such occasions. "Oh mam, it stings" I winced. "It has to sting to make it better," she said. Soon, I was out to playing again with my pals, sporting my golden brown wounds and feeling like a brave wounded soldier. "It was nowt, didn't hurt", I bragged.

Earlier, I mentioned Tommy Neasham, who was a blacksmith at the store, we used to live near him. I thought that Tommy must be the strongest man in the world. He was short and stocky with immense muscular arms, like a weight lifter. I don't recall seeing him without his grin and a twinkle in his eye. He was always full of fun and would joke with us – brought himself down to our level.

As lads, we would often go around to the blacksmiths' shop, in the works yard, just beyond the stables. The large wooden doors were always propped wide open, summer and winter alike, to dispel the smoke and styth, especially when he was shoeing horses, which was most of the time. We would lean against the wall opposite and gaze in wonder, into that hive of industry.

The store had about twenty horses, as the horse drawn cart was still the main means of delivery, although motor vehicles were used on the longer journeys, between the many outlying branches. What with all of these horses and those stabled in the various outlying branches, there was plenty of work for four blacksmiths. Not only did they make and fit horse shoes, they made the iron tyres for cart wheels which were built in the nearby wheelwrights' shop. Besides the blacksmiths, there was usually an apprentice and a labourer or blacksmith's striker as he was known. He was a deceptively strong and wiry man, old Harry. Not an ounce of fat on him. It was always something of a thrill to hear the ringing of the hammer on the steel anvil and to watch Tommy fashion a shoe from a straight piece of iron bar. First, the heating in the furnace, kept hot with small coals and a forced air draught. Checking the iron now and again for temperature, by a quick withdrawal with his tongs, before lunging back into the heat.

Shirt sleeves rolled up, always wearing a cloth cap, steel capped boots and leather apron, that's how I recall Tommy. Exercising his great skill on that hot iron bar, imposing his will upon it, hammering, bending, eyeing, reheating. Clang, clang, clang, clang, as the anvil rang out – wanting to be a church bell.

For the heavy hammering and shaping, old Harry would stand at the opposite side of the anvil, in readiness. His sledge hammer raised, one hand grasping the haft near the end and the other near the head. Holding his work with tongs on the anvil, Tommy would tap the appropriate spot with his hand hammer, as a signal to Harry. The blow of the sledge would descend on that precise spot, once only, then back to the raised position. It was fascinating to watch this team effort – the master craftsman, dictating the force and direction required, by his hand hammer tapping and the accurate delivery by the striker. Sparks flew outwards and upwards and sweat dripped from chins and noses, onto the stone cobbles below. Tap-clang, tap-clang, tap-clang, until the iron was wrought into shape to Tommy's satisfaction. Then the punching of the holes for studs and nails ready for the first fitting. Shoes were turned out in a variety of sizes and hung like bunches of bananas on the wall, ready for use.

Most of the horses were docile, from a docile occupation. These were not steeple chasers or hunters, but cart horses, plodders. Nevertheless, some of the younger horses were a bit mischievous. "Oh aye," Tommy would say, "yer've got to be very wary with some horses. The kickers and the biters. D'yer see these," he said, showing the white scars on his forearm, "them's horse bites, and Ar've had some nasty kicks an' all, but no bones broken," he laughed. "They don't try it on me any more, Ar kick back, and they get to respect me. They think twice about bitin' Tommy – save it for the apprentice," as he threw his head back laughing, and looking across the shop. "That right Billy?" Billy nodded without a smile.

A horse would be brought in for shoeing and tied to a ring on the wall. Tommy would always talk gently to the animal. "Yer see lads, yer should always be gentle, with slow movements. Put them at their ease, talk to them, coax them. Talk, and touch with your hands, so the horse can see yer. Slide yer hand down the horse to his leg," he demonstrated, then lift it. Never just go up and touch a horse on the flanks, they're very jumpy and nervous. If yer don't get their co-operation, yer'll never get them shod.

After stripping off the old shoe with his pincers and trimming the hoof, the apprentice would offer him a cold shoe to try for size. "Aye, that'll do lad, warm it up." Hot shoe on a spike in one hand, Tommy would offer this up to the hoof, which was clasped firmly between his leather aproned legs, before pressing it home, with the horn handle of his paring knife. Great billows of white smoke would squirt out and soon billow up into the shop and drift through the open doors. We would duck away if the smoke drifted towards us, to avoid the pungent smell, which was like nothing we had ever experienced before.

Once Tommy was satisfied with the fit of the shoe, then this was quenched in the trough with a hiss, and soon nailed into position through the edge of the hoof and

Tommy shoeing – master of his craft

trimmed around with a file. "There you are boy," as he released the horse's foot. Then the next and so on until the beast was newly shod and fit for service again. "There we are now," he would say, "another satisfied customer," as the horse was turned out and led away back to the stables. A master of his craft, he made it all look so easy.

When I got home, my mam would know where I'd been, immediately I entered the house. "Bah, Brian, yer've been down that blacksmiths again. Ar can smell that styth of horses' hooves, it's like sweaty socks."

CHAPTER 21

GRAMPS

Carl Robinson was a couple of years or so younger than me and a good mate. He lived with his mother in the terrace at the bottom of our street, next to the little shop. His grandparents lived in the end house, at the other side of the shop. Now Carl's dad was in the RAF and spent the war years in Canada and the Bahamas, lucky posting. His grandad was Harry – Gramps as he was always known. Carl spent most of his time at his grandparents' home, as his mother worked at the Odeon as an usherette.

There was a peculiar air raid shelter in Carl's back yard. This was a strong steel cage, where they could crawl for safety from falling masonry. It was more like a gigantic rusty rabbit pen, with its open mesh sides. The Robinsons were friendly with the butchers opposite, so always took refuge in their cellar during air raids.

I shall never forget the day that we were playing in that shelter, when we heard such shouting and commotion in the back way. A frantic cow appeared at their open yard gate. We later learned that it had made its getaway from a group that were being herded along the lane. The back way was a cul-de-sac, there was no way out. Carl's mam was in their kitchen, with the back door open. With no time to shut the door, she just dived into the pantry and closed the sliding door. The frightened beast bounded up the steps and into the kitchen. After careering about, knocking the table over and generally making a mess, it came out again, to retrace its path back to the herd. What excitement it was all over in a minute. What a shock for Mrs Robinson, it must have taken her ages to get over that experience.

Gramps had two allotments, a double. He was a very keen gardener and spent many long hours in his allotment and greenhouse, especially when he retired from his job as a painter with the council. A very keen trout fisherman, he would often take the bus to Witton-le-Wear, to fish in the river, in his big waders and his wicker fish basket slung around his neck. He would tell some tall tales about his fishing exploits, to fascinate us boys. We would sit and listen, wide eyed and open mouthed, just like trout. Often he would be seen walking to and from his allotment, pushing his wheelbarrow, with a cigarette dangling from the corner of his mouth. He always refered to his barrow as his, 'set of wheels' or 'bogie'.

Carl's mam sometimes would get complimentary tickets, which we lads used to go to the pictures, it saved sixpence. It didn't matter what film was on, we would watch anything that was going. The best thing that happened towards the end of the war, was when the Odeon started a Saturday morning Cinema Club, for children. We thought this was fantastic. The doors opened at half past nine, there were literally hundreds of youngsters queuing to get in. It cost sixpence downstairs and ninepence upstairs.

We soon learned, that if we purposely went late and joined the downstairs queue, then when downstairs was full, they would allow us upstairs at the same price. The proceedings started at ten o'clock. The manager came onto the stage, wearing evening dress and a black bow tie, to greet us all. We would sing a song that came up on the screen. This was the OCC song and the music would play. At the same time, a ping-pong ball bounced along the words on the screen, so that at least we could sing in time, if not in tune.

The song went like this:

We come a-long on Saturday Morning
Greeting everybody with a smile

To the O-DE-ON we have come
Now we're all together we can have some fun-Hoy!
Is every body happy – YES!
Do we ever worry – NO!
We're members of the OCC.

After singing this two or three times, there would be a competition of some kind, with volunteers from the audience, up on the stage. Once there was a ball bouncing contest, ball stotting, we called it. But we couldn't wait for the film and soon became restless and noisy.

There were whoops of delight when the competition was over. Time for the serial – Flash Gordon, with space ships, other worlds, Captain Zarkov, Ming the Merciless and other evil characters. Dale Arden was Flash Gordon's girl friend. He seemed to spend his life rescuing her from someone's evil clutches. The serial lasted about ten minutes. Poor Flash always ended up in a mess, he couldn't possibly escape. Then-WILL FLASH GORDON ESCAPE ALIVE? across the screen, TO BE CONTINUED – WATCH NEXT WEEK!

We could hardly wait to see if Flash had survived his ordeal. They played about a minute of the previous week's episode to recap on the story. We weren't silly and soon discovered that this was slightly different from the previous ending. Flash managed to escape. What a swizz, we felt a bit cheated, how they tried to fool us. Yet we still watched and followed the story each week, with great enthusiasm and excitement.

Then there was an interval to change the spools, before the main feature, usually a cowboy film. Gene Autrey, Roy Rogers, Hopalong Cassidy, what a magnificent world of make believe. If the film snapped which was not uncommon, then pandemonium would break out. Catcalls, whistles and stamping of feet. We were uncontrollable until the film started again. This produced instant silence.

When the show was over, you could see droves of boys galloping out of the Odeon in different directions, every one on horseback, whacking thighs and whooping as they went, "Giddup Trigger, giddup Silver." Some were Indians, with hands flapping over mouths, making loud, 'Indian noises.'

The air was thick with arrows and gunsmoke in Tenters Street, when the Odeon loosed.

There was a man whose job it was to keep us in order and keep us quiet if we made a noise during the performance. This man wore a uniform and a cap like a bandmaster. He was severe, with a loud booming voice, like a regimental sergeant major. His name was Bob Booth. We called him Big Bob, the chief chucker out. Would have you outside as soon as look at you, and no argument. You just did as he bid, to avoid a thick ear.

Once when Carl was talking loudly during the show. Big Bob descended on him with his searchlight torch. "Hey you, get out" he bawled. Carl stared at him, brazen faced. "You can't put me out," he protested, "my mother's Elsie Robinson," Carl was very smug, "Aye and me uncle Cliff's the assistant manager!" Bob was taken aback and didn't pursue the matter further. He knew on which side his bread was buttered!

Gramps had an old bus on his allotment, at least this was the bodywork of a bus, no chassis, no wheels, no engine just wooden bodywork, with windows all round. He used the old bus, as a potting shed for hanging up his onions and other plants that had to be dried out. There were clusters of large cabbage like leaves, tied with raffia and hung from nails, brown dry leaves. We discovered from Gramps, that these were tobacco plants. Ho-ho, great stuff this, what a discovery. We soon rolled some of the dry leaves into a tight pencil-like roll, a homemade cigar. The smoke was not like the fag ends we would sometimes puff, but strong and obnoxious. This ended in a lot of coughing and spluttering. That was the one and only experiment with home made cigars. Gramps only used these, we found, to eke out his rations, by mixing it with his pipe baccy.

We never had a dog in our family, despite pleas to my mam and dad. Nor did Carl. He and me would often stand and gaze longingly at the puppies in our local pet shop. "Herdmans have got some canny little puppies in mam", I would say, "oh can't we get one? Ar'll take it for walks and look after it." The answer was always an emphatic, "No"! She knew from the rabbits episode that the idea was not to be encouraged. Carl had a more subtle plan. When he'd saved enough pocket money, I went with him into Herdmans to buy a dog collar and lead. That was a crafty move on his part, a good lead in, as they say. His mam finally gave in and he was allowed to have a puppy, a golden retriever. What a cruel twist, he only had it for a day, it ran straight out onto the road past his mam and was knocked down by a car and killed. The poor little thing never even had a name, and Carl had to be content with white mice.

Gramps had a shed in his back yard where he bred hundreds of white mice. These were quite tame and he would sometimes close the door and let a few out for Carl to play with. They would creep all over him, sniffing the air and exploring. An adventure for all, including me. We would play for hours under the table in his gran's house, with toy soldiers and tanks. She was very kind. "What would you lads like to eat?" Wowie and scran was our favourite. At home I would often just have sugar with my bread, instead of treacle, especially when our jam ration had run out. You could just dip your buttered bread in the sugar basin, crunchy, sweet and delicious.

Carl – mouse boy

Another shop in Bishop, that held great fascination for us lads, was a pawn shop called Kenairs – you could tell by the three brass balls hanging over the door. Towards the end of the war, they started dealing in army surplus equipment, billy cans, khaki water bottles, haversacks and the like. What really fascinated us was the tent that was unrolled and displayed in the shop window, with its folding wooden poles. This was a bivouac tent. 'Ex US Army', the sign said, 'Sleeps Two, Only 32/6d.' I saved my pocket money and my casual earnings for weeks, even sold my stamp album, such was my determination to buy that tent. Carl and me would gaze into that window with longing, dreaming of camping adventures.

Finally, the day arrived when I had saved enough money and I went to call for Carl."Are yer comin' with us, to get the bivvy"?, as it had become familiarly known. Off we hurried to Kenairs to get the tent, and bring it excitedly home. Our sitting room had no carpet or lino, just bare boards, ideal for putting up a tent. My mam agreed and we soon found some nails in the cellar, to use as tent pegs. Up went the folding wooden poles and out came the white guy ropes. In went the nail tent pegs.

The tent was long and low, designed for the jungle. Stencilled on the side in black lettering were the words 'US ARMY', so that the Jap snipers could make no mistake! To our surprise and dismay, no matter how we buttoned and unbuttoned, and changed around the two parts of the bivvy, it soon became clear that this tent was open at one end, with a row of metal buttons. The other end went to a point. My mam went to complain. However, those were the days when the customer had few rights and she was unsuccessful in getting my money back. Mr Kenair had all the answers. "Oh, these tents button together in pairs, you'll need another, or you could always hang a bit of curtain over the end". And that's what we did. Imagine people putting up with that treatment nowadays. My dad didn't get involved, he knew it would be a complete waste of time and effort.

Roy Branch, the one with the hens, who lived out at Lands, had an old Morris Eight and would often call on us during his weekly trips into Bishop. "Wi there's plenty of room in my fields, if you lads want to camp", he offered. "Mind you, yer won't need an alarm clock. T'ard cock'll weken yer up in't mornin' " he laughed. We soon got ourselves organised, with a list of things to take camping and began to make preparations for our adventure. By the time we got kitted out, it was towards the end of the school summer holiday and we caught the old bus to the foothills of the Himalayas – about ten miles away.

Roy showed us where we could pitch our tent, at the top of his field near the pond, and this was soon done. The only thing I recall of our two day expedition, was walking to the village in the early morning with a milk can, only to find that everyone was still asleep. We learned from a group of pitmen returning home, black from work, that it was just after five o'clock. So we went back to our tent to get some more sleep.

There was this old gadgie, Mr Moffatt, who lived in Etherley Lane not far from the bottom of our street. He was a very old man in fact, with a bushy beard and always wore a black bowler hat. His whiskers were dark grey and tinged with nicotine around his moustache. No wonder, he always smoked a pipe which he only removed to spit. Men spat, we lads would spit, thought we were clever. Buses had notices up which said, 'No Spitting' or 'Spitting Not Allowed'. We knew his home very well, as he had a rotten tree stump in his garden. This was a plentiful source of dry and crumbling rotting wood, known locally as, 'touchwood'. We would make touchwood burners, especially in the winter months. Some lads made their burners from an old treacle tin with holes punched in and a wire carrying handle. Once lit, the tin would be swung around in great circles to make it glow red, for warming hands. Our touchwood burners were the best, made of clay from the rec clay pit. Formed into a brick shape, you would hollow this out with a knife and put holes in each end with a match stick. When you got the touchwood lit, you would blow and blow to make it glow red or charge along with it held at shoulder height, to drive air through the holes. The clay soon dried and you had a perfect hand warmer, with that never-to-be-forgotten smell, of hot drying clay and burning touchwood.

Old Mr Moffatt was coming along the lane one day, head

bent, at the kerb edge. We soon realised that he was look-ing for fag ends or dumps as we called them. Filter ciga-rettes were rarely smoked, so these dumps were all tobac-co. "Hey, do you lads want to make some pocket money?" We nodded. "Find me some good dumps for me pipe and Ar'll pay yer for them". Off we went, enthusiastically, armed with a brown paper bag apiece. We scoured the gut-ters of the town for fag ends. It took us all afternoon to fill our bags. We knocked on his door to offer our tobacco gleanings. His eyes lit up when he saw the bulging bags. "Wi, lads, Ar should get some good baccy out o' this lot". Taking the precious bags, he carefully placed them on a shelf, inside the porch, reached into his pocket and pro-duced two threp'ny pieces, one for each of us. We said, "Oh thanks" and off we went, disappointed. "All afternoon for a threp'ny didler" I said. "Howay and see if the fish shop's open," said Carl.

I don't remember Donnie's dad working. He was a sick man, always coughing and wheezing like a concertina with burst bellows. He would inhale something for his asthma, Potters Asthma Cure. Donnie's mam was an ailing woman, very pale complexion, grey hair and blue lips. She had a heart condition and always poorly. She died when he was about eleven and his dad was left to bring him up, with his young sister. His dad would sometimes take us to the pictures, usually the Kings Hall. The Kings, to us. We always sat downstairs, as these were the cheapest seats. The lop house, was an unkind name for the Kings, they said it was loppy, but it was the customers really that were loppy. The cheaper the seats, the more likely you were to be bitten by a flea. The pit stalls were right up against the screen, you could crick your neck watching, but very cheap at thre'pence. We never went upstairs, that was really posh, all the courting couples would go up there to snog during the performance. Saturday night was the night for snogging in the pictures. Of course my mam wouldn't let me go there on a Saturday night, in case I saw something untoward. "You're not going tonight, all that slopping and kissing going on, ugh"! So that was an end to it. "What's the harm", I won-dered, "they were only copying what their favourite film stars seemed to be doing all the time".

CHAPTER 22

MISS MILLERS

When we had first moved into No 21, old Mrs Hardwick lived next door, between us and the Winskill sisters. She never left the house much and I shall never forget the day she died. My mam remarked one Saturday morning, "Fred, do you think Mrs Hardwick's alright, her curtains are still drawn?", and this was about ten o'clock. He knocked and hammered on the front door, to no avail. Then he got our steps from the corner, a roofed cubby hole in the yard, next to the lavatory and popped these against the dividing wall between our yards. He was soon over the wall and opened her back gate. After, knocking on the back door, with no response, he said, "She's maybe collapsed or something. Ar'll see if Ar can get in through the landing window." There was a slated pitched roof over the single storey scullery. The landing window could be reached by climbing up the slates. Up he went, like a cat, the window had frosted white glass with swirling patterns of leaves, there were small panes of red glass, little squares in the corners. We had the same sort of landing window, which made the sun cast coloured patterns down the stairs. A pair of pliers were produced from his back pocket, which he used to break a glass pane to reach the window catch. Click, the window was soon slid open and my dad slithered inside.

Then his head appeared, "She's on the bedroom floor, dead. Go and fetch Mrs Palmer and Ar'll go for Sergeant Dexter." Mrs Palmer was an enormously fat woman in our street, she'd been a nurse in her younger years and was skilled in laying out the dead. She was always sent for, when anyone died. After Mrs Hardwick's death, the house was sold and the Miss Millers moved in. They were Jean and Flo, who had come from nearby mining village, to a smaller house as their parents had died. Their two batchelor brothers George and Fred had jobs away from home. These were two genteel ladies, who had a private school education. They were an artistic and talented family. Their father had been the manager of Leeholme Colliery for a number of years, quite an exalted position in the community.

We soon found that they had another brother who lived with them. They were his guardians, his nursemaids and devoted servants. He was Bertie, born an imbecile and although he was middle aged at that time, his mental age was only a few months. The Miss Millers kept Bertie hidden from the outside world. Nobody was allowed to see him, except of course the doctor, if he was ill. Bertie was molly-coddled, always well wrapped up, in case he caught a cold. He was fed on the best they could provide and had to be nursed like a baby, wasn't toilet trained. You can imagine the devotion of those sisters. When she was on her death bed, their mother had made her two daughters promise that they would always look after Bertie when she was gone and they vowed to do so. My dad was so kind to the Miss Millers, they took him into their confidence. They sometimes needed some moral support, as well as relying on him to do odd jobs around the house. They allowed him to see Bertie. He wasn't grotesque, as he had imagined, but just vacant looking, very small with short legs. His only means of speaking was an "Aag-aag" noise, shouted out. Bette and me soon got to know his voice, as he was in the back bedroom next to ours. We got used to the sound of Bertie calling and soon learned to ignore it. My dad said that he was just like a little old man, but would swing on the edge of the table, like a little bairn might. Always buttoned up tight, he wore a balaclava helmet to keep him warm. With no conscious control of his bowels he spent his life in nappies. Oh those poor girls, how could their mother have imposed such a thing on them. They had such potential as artistic and intelligent people and would have made good wives and mothers.

They were ashamed of Bertie, ashamed for the world outside to see him. What a relief for them on the day that my dad met him. "Hello Bertie. My word, what a grand little chap you are", and he stroked his head with feeling. "Do you think he's not too bad Mr Joslin, we've been worried about you meeting him", said Flo. "Don't worry honey, Bertie's alright, he's a grand little feller. You can tell that he's loved and well cared for. You're doing a grand job", reassured my dad. "Aag-aag," grunted Bertie as if he knew.

Flo had a job in Jones's ladies outfitters in Bishop, but Jean stayed at home all the time because of Bertie. It was only on the very rare occasion that they both left the house. "Bertie is never any trouble", said Jean, "he's no bother." She explained how he would never leave his bedrooom on his own, especially when they left the feather duster propped against the wall by the door. He was terrified of the feather duster, wouldn't venture anywhere near it. The Miss Millers had no electricity in their house, only gas light and they kept a good fire on in winter, to keep their little charge warm.

My dad, who was always being helpful, fixed them an electric lamp in their kitchen by drilling a hole between our cupboard at the side of the fireplace and their cupboard. A flex was passed through this hole and he fixed them a table lamp with a switch, so that they had a light. The other end of the flex was plugged into a socket by our kitchen window. This worked out fine and as it was only a sixty watt lamp, he didn't charge for the electricity. This went on for a long time, until my dad discovered that brother George, when he came home for the weekend, would connect an electric fire to this lamp. I seem to remember that there were some cross words over the wall, on the subject and my dad unplugged the flex. I don't think that the Miss Millers would have taken advantage of what was a kindly act. George was different, I remember him as a sombre and grumpy man, never much to say, he used to like a drop of booze and would come swaying up the street from the bus stop. He was a Dog and Gun man.

Jean was a talented musician, a pianist, who got great pleasure from playing the piano in their sitting room. With only a wall between us, we would often hear her playing the piano. I recall only one tune, from all she played, "We'll Gather Lilacs in the Spring Again". Perhaps she would dream of the young man she could never marry, a sad song for this lady. Oh what a wasted life, all for an imbecile brother, whose quality of life was almost nil in my view, so sad.

Flo had a gentleman friend, although he never came to their house. Leonard, was the licensee of a public house in Bishop and she would enjoy a drink with him. They also played tennis in the rec. She had a tennis raquet with a fish tail handle, I'd never seen the likes before or since, always kept it clamped in a frame. One winter she went down with 'flu' and was very ill. My dad asked the doctor to visit her. Doctor Wardle arrived and went upstairs to examine her. When he came downstairs he prescribed some medication to see her through the attack, which by that time had passed the crisis. My dad explained that poor Jean was absolutely washed out, sleeping on her feet, what with looking after her sister and Bertie. The doctor remarked to her that she didn't look too well herself and prescribed a tonic for her. "You must get some rest, your sister is past the critical stage and her temperature is coming down".

He looked at Bertie, sitting there, tucked up in his chair near the fire. Jean had gone into the scullery to make a cup of tea. "You see him, Mr Joslin. Strong as an ox. He'll see these two off, he should be in a home, but they won't hear of it. I wish you could persuade them. It would be better for everyone." "Ar'll keep an eye on them doctor, Mrs Joslin is going into town to get the medicine. When the time is opportune, Ar'll try to make them see sense." But he knew that they would never agree to such a plan.

CHAPTER 23

CHRISTMAS

Often, during the school holidays, we would stay at gram-ma's in Houghton-le-Spring, aunty Mattie and uncle Jack were nearby. They had Alan and Marian, my cousins. Alan was about two years older than me, Marian was younger than our Bette.

When Alan was very small, about a year old he contract-ed tuberculosis in his right forefinger. My dad told me later that he had probably caught the infection from gram-ma's second husband, Roger, who was riddled with the disease. He was often taken to the sanitorium for long spells of treatment. Poor little Alan, had to go to the Sunderland Royal Infirmary, where they amputated his finger to pre-vent the spread of the disease, as there was no known cure then. A neat little stump stood alongside his three fingers and he soon learned to cope. He would sit and twine his golden curls with his middle finger. This was always when sitting thinking or daydreaming. Come to think of it, I had, and still have the same habit, using always the middle fin-ger of my right hand, perhaps something in our common genealogy.

I went around quite a lot with Alan and his mates, a bit of a wild bunch. We would go to the baths, that is the swimming baths, on a Saturday morning. There was no swimming pool at Bishop, so it was a great novelty and a great treat, to be going to the swimming baths. These were at Lambton, a pit village, it took about five minutes on the bus. Nobody seemed to care if you could swim or not, there was no one to teach you to swim, you just made your own way. The two outstanding things I remember about Lambton Baths, were the cold water and the presence of rough and noisy big lads, who took a delight in throwing you into the water, especially if they found that you couldn't swim. There was no supervision, the conditions were spartan, but still the water was warmer than the North Sea, the only other place where we bathed. I recall shivering as we got ourselves dried and dressed to go back to aunty Mattie's.

During the war years there were British Restaurants set up by the government in most towns. This was where people could get square meals, at reasonable prices. There was such an establishment in Houghton, in a Nissen hut. Aunty Mattie would often send us off to the pictures, to the Colliseum, 'The Collie,' "Then you can get your dinners at the British Restaurant. The Colly was a poor man's Odeon, but who cared, the pictures were just as good, even had Flash Gordon and Hopalong Cassidy, just like home.

The British Restaurant had to seen to be believed, it was what you might call basic. There was the inevitable queue along the serving counter, with no choice of menu. What did you expect in wartime?. Usually there was pea soup, like dishwater, warm dishwater mind you. There were always mashed potatoes, lumpy of course, then some crusty meat pie of doubtful content, plenty of gristle that you couldn't swallow. The inevitable mushy peas or dark green stringy cabbage, were all drenched in a ladle of luke-warm gravy. To hungry lads, it smelled very appetising, fit for a king. There were trestle tables with oil cloth covers and wooden forms to sit on. Rough and ready, but it only cost sixpence. The sweet would probably be spotted dick, with lumpy custard or tapioca with a dollop of red jam in the middle. Who could wish for more?.

We would go back to gram-mas via the pit heap, which loomed over and dominated the town and try to find some tarry tout to light and swing around our heads to make it glow red at the end. This was a tar impregnated hemp, which had formed the core of steel ropes, used in the pit. There were many such pieces of rope around the pit yard and on the pit heap, that were old and rusted away, leaving the tout core easy to get at. This would glow when you lit it, like a cigarette, would burn for hours like a slow fuse on a stick of dynamite. Some of the lads smoked fags or tabs, as they were known locally. "Arv'e pinched a Woodbine out of me dar's pocket. D'yer want a drag"?, offered Billy, who was usually amongst our gang who lived on the Homelands Estate. Then we would go down by the pig crees, to smoke and have a game of muggles.

When it got dark we could see the strings of barrage balloons around Sunderland, with their floppy dumbo ears, discouraging dive bombing. Often we could see search lights criss crossing the night sky during an air raid, looking for the German raiders. We could hear the thud of bombs and see flashes in the sky, being not far from the coast. Houghton was not deliberately bombed, but there were sometimes stray bombs. We would go out into the woods and fields looking for souvenirs, like shrapnel or spent cartridges from machine guns.

Uncle Roger was called up into the RAF and was commissioned as a flying officer, a navigator. He spent most of the wartime in Canada, training Canadians to fly. Aunty Edith was in the ATS and stationed in Wrexham in North Wales, working on anti-aircraft guns. One of the Ack-Ack girls.

Alan's dad, my uncle Jack was a blacksmith at the pit. He always came home as black as a sweep and would greet me, "Hello bonnie lad" and always treated me kindly. He seemed to have a soft spot for me. I should think that Alan got little encouragement at school, at least if it was anything like our school. The standards were similar, by all accounts.

Marian was bright and intelligent as well as being pretty and grew up to be very attractive, like her mother. She had high aspirations, even when she was four, she wanted a horse to ride on. One Christmas, Santa brought her a hobby horse, a horse's head with a mane and reins, with a wooden pole and two wheels on the bottom. Marian was set up with this horse, Dobbin, she christened it. She loved that horse.

Edith had a nice bike and would let me have a ride, when we were visiting. This was the first two wheeler that I'd ridden and I soon got the hang of it, what a thrill. First she would ask me to blow the tyres up hard, which I soon did, with great enthusiasm. She was always encouraging, "Bah Brian, you're a good tyre pumper, Ar can never do them like that", as she tried to press her thumb into the tread. "You must have strong arms". This made me feel good, and I would pump all the harder.

Edith had a kind nature, I was happy when she was around. On a later visit to gram-mas my mam and dad took me to see uncle John and aunty Jenny, just a few minutes walk away. This was to be a very special surprise for me. Uncle John was waiting at their back gate when we arrived, just enjoying a cigarette. He was wearing a great big grin. "Hello", he greeted us "nice to see you again, howay in, Jenny's just makin' a cup of tea". He couldn't wait to show me his surprise. "Come and see what Ar've got for you Brian", as he took my arm and led me into their scullery. There was a lovely bike, just like Edith's, propped against the wall. "This is my old bike, Ar've cleaned it all up like and oiled it. It's for you to take home". I couldn't believe my eyes, that I should have my own bike, but there was something different about this bike. I studied it. There was no saddle. This was no problem, uncle John had wrapped a thick layer of sacking around the place where the saddle should be and made a comfortable seat.

He took me out in the back lane to have a ride. I was thrilled to have such a grand bike and would be the envy of my mates when I got home, nobody had a bike in our street. I shall never forget the joy of proudly wheeling my bike to the railway station at Fence Houses. It had to travel in the Guard's Van.

Aunty Edith was my favourite, so warm and kind, we always had a lot of fun when Edith was around. One of the most exciting Christmases during the war, was when she came to stay with us. She was home on leave at the time. We had a clothes rail, in our kitchen, a wooden one, for hanging washing on, to air. This was hung from the ceiling by two iron brackets and must have been twelve feet long.

The rail, my mam called it, "There's a dry towel on the rail" or "Fred, Ar've ironed your shirt, it's on the rail". This particular Christmas 1944 I think, because I would be about nine years old, my dad had acquired a set of coloured lights. Christmas tree lights were not available during the war, nor were spare bulbs. But these were not Christmas tree lights, oh no; much bigger and more grand. These were real mains lamps on a string of cable and had been used for a shop display before the war. My dad had got these from his friend Stan, who was the foreman electrician at the store.

When he brought in this cardboard box one day from work, he showed me the contents. How I marvelled, I'd never seen the likes in my life, a tangled coil of cable with lampholders and an assortment of coloured lamps. They were red, yellow, green and blue, big bulbs, like the one in our kitchen. He soon had this plugged in, the lamps inserted one by one, just laid along the kitchen floor. My mind boggled at these colours.It would be a week or so before Christmas, so my dad hung the lights up. What better place than on our 'line'? They were strung in festoons along the wooden line and connected from the central light. When he switched on, our kitchen was immediately transformed into a world of Christmas magic. We had a few other decorations and a small tree, but to me, the lights were the ultimate. I imagined that Santa's home must be something like this. The weather turned very cold in that week before Christmas and we had some snow, not a lot. There was ice everywhere, unrelenting, there was no thawing, even in the daytime with the weak winter sun.

The news that Edith would be coming, made me feel glad and everything was just perfect. Oh, what a festive time this would be. As Christmas approached, there has been the weeks of anticipation and preparation in our house. The making of the Christmas cake was a memorable event. My mam would build up a store of ingredients over the months, eeked from our food ration. She would collect currants, raisins, sugar, flour, candied lemon peel and shining glazed cherries. There would be butter, eggs, spices and who knows what, to go into that cake.

Mam and me would sit up to the blue checked, bleached

*That Christmas, Edith was coming
and everything would be perfect*

white oil cloth covered kitchen table. "Now stop picking that", she would say, as I poked at the cracks in the oil cloth, where it creased over the table corner. "You're supposed to be helping me to make the cake, not picking bits off the table cover". We would seemingly spend hours cutting raisins in half and removing the seeds. "You don't want pips in your Christmas cake", she would declare, "just good fruit". As we worked away with scissors, cutting the raisins, the glazed cherries and lemon peel, I would lick my sweet and sticky fingers with delight and I must admit the occasional glazed cherry went missing, delicious. Then there was the mixing and blending of the ingredients and preparing the oven tins. She had two large round baking tins. These were indentical in size, twin tins, you might say. Why? Well, she always made a pair of cakes, one for Christmas and one for the New Year. So the tins were prepared. They were black and burnt with use and had loose round bottoms. These tins were lined with greaseproof paper that she cut from a sheet, so that the cakes wouldn't stick.

My dad had moved the ancient gas oven from the cellar to a place at the top of the cellar steps. When this was lit, it had an unmistakable, but homely smell of coal gas and hot grease which soon drifted into the kitchen and pervaded the whole house. Once the mixture had been put into the tins, my mam would smooth it and paint the top with a white of an egg and milk to give a nice finish. It always took several hours to bake these cakes and towards the end, she would open the oven door and reach in with a knitting needle to prod and test. "When the needle comes out clean, then it's done, ready to take out". The smell of hot grease and gas was overwhelmed by the mouth watering smell, the baking cakes, aromatic spices and fruits. At last one cake was ready and taken out to stand cooling. The other moved higher up the oven, to finish off. Some people, I heard would make their Christmas cakes, months before, so that they would mature and gain flavour, like vintage wine. Ours were made two or three weeks before Christmas and suited us fine. No time to mature, they had such a short, though merry life. There were no ground almonds to be had then, but semolina and almond essence worked into a paste made a very good substitute.

The wine for Christmas, was made from a small bottle of essence. This little bottle was square, with a round neck and a bright yellow label. 'Three Castles Green Ginger Wine Essence' was printed in black. It was very strong, very potent and the cork was sealed with red wax, to keep in the flavour. We had a large brown earthenware bowl, white inside, that she used for baking. The potion was opened and the rich brown contents were poured into this basin that had been filled with kettles of boiling water. Sugar was added and the whole lot stirred with a wooden spoon. The vapour made my eyes smart and water, such was the potency of this brew. When it had cooled, out would come the empty dandelion and burdock bottles that we had kept under the stairs and these were filled by means of a jug and tin funnel. They went back under the stairs, 'till Christmas.

My dad preferred Old Salt, to dandelion and burdock, a stronger taste, with a fisherman in sou-wester on the label, smoking a pipe. Although he never smoked or took strong drink. I think this only tasted like beer, not the real McCoy, a forerunner of Kaliber. What with the green ginger wine and the cake, this was one of the happiest memories of my childhood. Oh what bliss and on top of all that Santa was bringing me a chemistry set, my life would then be complete. Returning to school was a long way off.

It was Christmas Eve when Edith was expected. My dad and me were to meet her off the bus in the market place. Off we went, all wrapped up to keep warm. The sky was clear, the twinkling stars above with the ice below, winking back. There was hoar frost on the school railings, they were like ghostly icing sugar railings and looked unreal. Many things looked unreal at Christmas, a time of make believe, that had come true. The ice was slippery but we were sure footed, my dad always had plenty of studs in my shoes, to grip the ice in winter, saved your soles as well, and he was into soul saving. I recall standing in Bishop Market Place outside Doggarts, on that Christmas Eve. It was crisp and dry, everything in darkness except for the buses and cars with their masked lights, just slits to direct the light towards the ground.

There were walls of sandbags around the entrance to the Town Hall which was transformed into an Air Raid Wardens' Post. The shop windows were dark, not a chink of light and heavily taped in square patterns, to prevent splintering. Being Christmas eve, the bus from Durham was very late in arriving. It was a blue double decker, as it appeared round the bend and into the market place, squinting to see its way to the right bus stop, like a mole. Edith was smiling and looked smart in her uniform, waving from the dimly lit interior of blue light, very strange. We greeted her, with Merry Christmases all round, then linked our arms together as we headed up Bondgate towards home. Edith was a bundle of fun, a happy soul in my mind, laughing and joking, warm and affectionate. Her lovely singing accent, not Geordie but Sunderland, a subtle difference.

Pure Geordie land is north of the Tyne, whereas Sunderland is on the banks of the river Wear. Wearsiders and Tynesiders are from different tribes, they owe allegiance to separate and famous football teams. Newcastle may have had its Jackie Milburn, but Sunderland had its Bobby Gurney, both legendary figures and we were proud to be related by family to Bobby. Edith always had time to talk to me and was interested in what I was doing. She was a shining light in the dim world of those wartime days. I wished Edith could stay with us always, she brought such joy.

How strange when I think back, Christmas Eve and not a light in sight, apart from the stars. It's easy to forget how severe was the blackout. Dad on one side, Edith on the other, away we went slipping and slithering on the polished pavements, laughing with excitement. When we got home, there was an enormous coal fire and my mam made a pot of tea and cut the new Christmas cake, just to 'try it'. There were lots of news to exchange and lots of laughter. We were proud of our Christmas lights, which gave the kitchen a lovely warm glow. This was a Christmas to be remembered. By about nine o'clock, Bette and me had to go to bed. Santa would be coming tonight. The sooner we got to sleep the sooner we would wake up and it would be Christmas day.

CHAPTER 24

TRAUMAS, TATIES AND TROOPS

I went up into Mr Bull's class, the top class at our school, when I was ten. This was the big push for the eleven plus. The only problem was that Mr Bull pushed me backwards, rather than forwards, as he did with everyone else who was only of average ability. At least I wasn't a no-hoper. Those unfortunates were put on permanent rabbit duties and gardening. There was a handful of boys, a group that was considered to be beyond redemption. Understandably, these were boys from the Town Head or orphans from the Cottage Homes. Mr Bull's method of communicating with these, 'fatheads' as he termed them, was to bellow at the top of his voice, like his namesake, with the occasional cuffing across the ear. What did it matter anyway, they weren't going anywhere in life. Tests in class, were regularly conducted, in reading, writing and arithmetic. These always confirmed that these boys were numbskulls. How could they ever become anything else, there was no special teaching for them. The attitude was, that the class was much better, without these individuals and besides, if they'd a choice in the matter, they would prefer rural duties. At least they could dodge about and have a crafty smoke now and again, behind the rabbit shed.

I was never much good at sport, although I was obliged to play football and cricket. Football I hated, cricket was more tolerable, as I was quite a good hand at bowling. But I could do little with the bat. The ball was too fast for me to see, never mind hit. An embarrassing situation arose one playtime, when the headmaster Mr Siddle, joined in our game of cricket. He took the bat, presumably to show us lads how it should be done and went into the crease. I happened to be bowling at the time. You may understand that I was very nervous, and wished that I could have passed the ball to someone else. My bowling wasn't particularly fast and fancy spinners were not in my repertoire. Nevertheless I had remembered what my uncle John had taught me and my placing of the ball was accurate. Mr Siddle squared up in the crease, a formidable sight. "Come on then Joslin, what are you waiting for?" I bowled him clean out. Out for a duck! He coloured up, redder than his normal ruddy face. "Well done Joslin" he said, as he handed back the bat to us and sauntered casually away. There was no doubt in my mind, that he would get me for that, I wish I could have missed. My pals talked about it for years. "Remember that time you bowled old Fiddley out for a duck, just what that old bugger wanted".

Shortly after that incident I shall never forget the day I broke a picture. For some reason I had gone into a classroom one Friday dinner time. We were always supposed to be outside in the playground or the school field. There was a football on the floor, which had been got out of the sports cupboard and pumped up hard, in readiness for a game in the afternoon. I began to idly tap the ball up one of the aisles between the desks to the back wall and it came bouncing back. After a couple of times, the position of the ball was just right, perfect for a goal shot. I bunched it, couldn't resist it. Really, 'gave it some McIntyre', as we used to say. This was a shop in Bishop, that sold football boots. There was a picture of, 'The Young Walter Raleigh – Looking Out To Sea', high on that back wall. Alas! not high enough! The ball smashed the picture. Young Raleigh never noticed, as fragments of glass showered over the desks and floor. The sound was deafening and I could feel the blood draining from my already pale face.

Another lad, Malcolm Speed who was there, said that I turned a sickly shade of green. "Bloody hell Jos" he said "old Bully 'al 'ave a fit". My mind went numb with fear. This was a heinous crime and my punishment would be unthinkable. This was something that I couldn't undo, the die had been cast. You can imagine the buzz and chatter, when the class assembled. I stood at the front, waiting for Mr Bull to arrive. When he walked in, there was a deathly silence, as he glanced at the scene.

"Ar'm sorry sir", I volunteered, "but the ball just bounced and hit the picture". He looked around surveying the damage, peering over his spectacles as he did when he was angry. "Bounced! Bounced!", his voice rose to a screaming crescendo, "you mean you kicked it. You fathead," With that he delivered an almighty slap across my head with his open hand. My head rang like a church bell. "Hand out" he bellowed as he reached for his stick. He knew how to lay it on. Three of the best were delivered in quick succession. "Now the other," he shouted, and my left hand was treated likewise. "You're a fool Joslin, now go and get a brush and shovel from the caretaker and clean up this mess." I left the room, like a zombie, in a daze, head ringing and hands smarting. I nursed my hands under my armpits for relief, as I made my way to the boiler room, to find Mr Bramwell, who gave me a brush and dustpan and a cardboard box to put the glass in. My hands were throbbing with pain as I carefully swept up every last piece of broken glass, which I quietly deposited into the cardboard box. I felt that I was acting out a part, I might have been a ghost, Mr Bull just continued with the lesson, as I carried out my task. Holding the cardboard box, I made my way out of the classroom, to the boiler house and handed this over to Mr Bramwell. Another lesson learned.

October was a good month in the school term during the war, for this was when we were given two weeks holiday, to help with the potato harvest. Tatie picking was always a good chance to earn some pocket money, but it was hard work, backbreaking. We would arrange this, in the weeks prior to the holiday, by going to local farms, until we got our names on their list of labourers. Off we would set, bright and early to start picking at 7.30am. One year Carl

We caught the old bus to go tatie picking

and me were engaged at Blockitts Farm, about two miles from where we lived. That first cold October morning was a bit of a shock on the system, getting up before 7 o'clock and catching the old bus, each with a galvanised bucket slung over his shoulder. A few sandwiches and a large, corked medicine bottle full of milk, was all the sustenance which we required.

Dinner time was twelve 'til one o'clock. Then we carried on, until five o'clock. All the pickers gathered in the farm yard. There would be about twenty I suppose, all boys, this was not girls' work, but usually there were a couple of women. These were older women, of a roughish nature, hawker stock. They smoked cigarettes in public, which was not the done thing, perhaps they didn't care what people thought.

The farmer's wife, Mrs Blockitt, as I recall, was rather round and plump. She wore wellingtons and an old fawn coat, without a belt, which was always buttoned up to the neck. Definitely not the stereotyped jolly farmer's wife, but sour faced and unsmiling, the first woman I'd ever seen to wear a cap. Her beady grey eyes missed nothing. With one hand she led the horse and cart, the other sported a cane walking stick, which was used with great skill as a tatie pointer. "Come on everyone, we'd better get started". Mr Blockitt also wore a cap and had a hare lip. He drove the tractor towing the potato lifting machine. This had an arrangement of wheels with spring tines, like spokes that rotated and dug open the mound, throwing the white soil caked spuds into the air like pebbles off a beach.

Our local name for this machine was, 'tatie scratter'. Very descriptive, like a pair of crazed terriers travelling along the mound, relentlessly digging, as if their lives depended upon it. Mrs Blockitt distributed hessian sacks from the cart and we followed the scratter, like gulls following a plough. At first it was thought to be fun, as us lads dashed and darted about, filling our buckets with spuds, then emptying them into the sacks.

As the morning wore on, we became weary and our pace slowed. The women never flagged, just lit another fag and pressed on, with seemingly boundless energy. The encouraging voice of Mrs Blockitt urged us on, "Look you've missed one, look there, pointing with her stick. Come on, we'll never get the crop in at this rate!" – she was a slave driver. At about 10 o'clock, one of the farm hands arrived with two massive cans of tea and we all had a rest in the dyke back. This was really working, like my dad, and I was wearing a pair of his old bib and brace overalls, tucked into my wellies. The first day seemed very long, as we wearily trailed back to the farmyard to receive our wages. We were given half a crown each for our day's labour and learned that the two women pickers were paid 4/6d, which was fair, they were good workers and didn't lark about.

The usual practice was that you could take a bucket of potatoes home each day, as a bonus. Mrs Blockitt had a different scheme, whereby you could take the biggest potato you could find. There was great activity in scrabbling about amongst the heap, to find large spuds. However, we soon learned that the bigger the tatie, the more likely it was to be rotten inside. This was a bit of a mean trick we thought, so we soon learned to lob a few spuds over the dyke, to be picked up on our way home. We had soon beaten the system. After one week, we'd had enough and were exhausted, but there were always plenty of others to fill our places and to learn the lessons that we old timers had learned.

Some of my mates were great swearers, I would sometimes participate, we thought we were so clever and grown up. As lads we would brag about our swearing. Arnie would declare, "Ar swear in the house, does thoo?". "Ar swear at me fatha" responded Stoney. I would join in, "Me an' all, me fatha says nowt". One day, my mam had heard some choice words flying about in our back street. Stoney was the culprit and she went out to reprimand him. "Bah, Ar've never heard such language. You're a brazant lot, you want to get away back to your own street, we're not used to that sort of language around here." "Well you should be, your Brian swears", came the reply. She looked shocked and turned on me. "Do you swear"? My denial was immediate and emphatic "No mam, honestly", "Wi aye he does" said Stoney, "he's always swearin'." "Get in this house," my mam shouted, as she clashed me around the ears, towards our open gate.

I never heard my dad swear and my mam only once, but that was my fault. I don't know what I'd been up to, but recall her chasing me around the kitchen table with a sweeping brush. She was frustrated at not being able to catch me. "You little bugger," she blurted. "Now you've made me swear, it's all because of you, you'd make a parson swear".

Once I chalked some rude words on the wall about Evelyn who lived out our back. She was so shocked and annoyed, and went and told my mam. "Your Brian's been writing rude words on the wall about me. And another thing, he smokes cinammon". She must have felt good when she got that off her chest. I got a good dressing down and was made to rub out my chalkings. It was true, we did buy sticks of cinnamon at the chemists. They made good cigars, or you could eat them if you wanted to.

The Eden Theatre stood on the corner where Princes Street joined Newgate Street, the main street in Bishop.

This was a meeting point for one and all. "See yer at the Thee-ater corner". There could be no misunderstanding, you couldn't miss it. In Bishop, this was always pronounced, 'thee-ater,' a very distinctive building in the town and many famous music hall artists over the years, had trod its boards, George Robey, G.H.Elliott, the chocolate coloured coon and countless others. I remember Wee Georgie Wood. There were shows staged throughout the war. As lads we always went into the gallery which was only sixpence. The rows of seats there were so steep, you sometimes thought you were going to fall down and over the bannister rail. Once when my cousin Alan was staying with us, my mam gave us some money to go to the pictures. We had intended going to the Kings, but for some reason, we decided to go to the theatre, up in the gods.

This was a variety show. The only act I recall was a striptease, where a glamorous blonde went behind a screen and the compere auctioned her clothes. "How much am I bid for her stockings?" "A dollar, someone would volunteer". The stockings would be thrown over the screen and then passed down to the bidder, to the delight and cheers of the audience. Then her dress and brassiere likewise, the tension was mounting as the garments were flung over the screen. "How about a pair of panties, how much?" "Half a nicker", hollered some stooge. This was beginning to look like a put up job. She soon ran out of garments. "How much am I offered to remove the screen?" The bidding soon reached a pound. "Right, a pound it is ladies and gentlemen", and with a roll of drums the screen was pulled aside. Only to reveal a man who was the spitting image of Adolph Hitler, with black hair, moustache and jackboots. He was booed loudly as he goose stepped away into the wings. My mam was vexed when she found out where we had been, she'd heard about this show and considered it unsuitable for children. I overheard her telling Mrs Robertson next door. "Do you know, our Brian and Alan have been to see that blue show at the thee-ater, they shouldn't let children in". I didn't understand what she was talking about.

The store backway, as it was known, ran along behind the theatre. This was so named because it led to the back of the Co-op. This backway, was sandwiched between the railway line and Newgate Street and formed a large wedge shaped piece of waste land, where there was an electrical substation. My dad would sleep there on a camp bed, when he was on firewatching duty. The army arrived during one night, and by morning, this piece of land was full of tanks and lorries, with lots of soldiers carrying guns. I think this was part of an armoured division and in preparation for D-Day. There were guards on duty, who would chase us lads if we got too near. Also, there were women hanging around the store backway, with red lips and rosy cheeks, scrounging cigarettes off the soldiers. I could never understand why they were always around or where they came from. After a few days, the army was gone and so were the smoking, 'troop carriers'.

Immediately next to the Eden Theatre there was a group of slum dwellings known as Gregory's Yard, with a narrow passage between, linking to the main street. This was a filthy place, you could smell it when you passed by. The urchins who lived there were barefoot and dirty, worse than the Town Head bairns. These were people to be pitied, they seemed to have no will to lift themselves out of the mire and the squalor, just festered there and bred like rabbits. These properties were owned by a local well known businessman, a pillar of the Chapel – what hypocrisy. But no worse than the Church of England, who were the landlords of many city slums. How would they explain that away on Judgement Day?

There were always plenty of other soldiers around, during the war, with army camps nearby. In the forecourt of Bishop Railway Station there was the LNER Institute, where dances were sometimes held. As lads we would play around the station, riding on four wheeled bogeys, used for parcels or running onto the bridges to drop pebbles down the funnels of passing trains, to watch them fly up into the air again. We would often walk along the black path or lovers lane, as it was known, which ran from the station by the rec fence, to Latherbrush bridge. There would sometimes be soldiers walking hand in hand with girls from the dance. One summer night, when the rec was closed, Arnie, Howard and myself were trying to climb over the railings as a short cut home. There were two soldiers walking by with girls in long ballgowns, one pink, one blue. One said "I'll soon get you over there lads, come here". With that, he picked me up in his great strong arms and with one movement, swung me up and over the railings. In a moment, I was in the grass at the other side. My two mates followed in like fashion. I think Tommy was just showing off his strength to his girl.

At other times we would see soldiers and girls, rolling about in the deep grass, in the bottom field of the rec. They were kissing like on the films. It must have been very warm, because sometimes the soldiers would have their shirt tails out, just flapping about in the breeze. I once told my mam that we had seen a soldier and a woman, rolling about in the grass, down the rec. She became quite speechless and made no comment. The next day I heard her at the front door talking to Mrs Robertson. "Eeh!, do you know, them soldiers have been courting in the grass, they wouldn't be doing 'that' in the rec, surely? Ar don't know what things are comin' to. The sooner they've all gone, the better. There was never anything like that going on before the war." How naive she must have been. Sometimes we would find white balloons lying about and blew them up. My mam said, "Yer want nothing playing around with those things, you might catch something. They use those at Aycliffe for tests." Lots of people travelled by train to Aycliffe, to work in the munitions factory and they would spill out of long trains at the end of the day. It seemed logical that they used these balloons in some sort of tests. She had a very inventive mind, especially when it came to explaining away anything connected with sex. Part of our learning about life, was gleaned from writings and drawings on the walls of the station lavatories, very educational.

The Lady Eden Cottage Hospital was the only hospital in Bishop, apart from the Workhouse, which had its own hospital wing. This all changed during the war. Preparations were being made to receive the German wounded prisoners of war, by the building of prefabricated hospital wards. This complex was built on the land which adjoined the Workhouse or The Poor Law Institute as it was known. When the new hospital was complete and equipped, it was surrounded by high barbed wire fences, with sentry posts.

Shortly after D-Day, the new wards began to be occupied, with soldiers guarding the gates. The majority of these German prisoners were not seasoned regular soldiers, but older men and young boys in their teens, who had been drafted into the army by the Nazi regime.

As the war progressed through Europe, the hospital was extended and filled to capacity. We would sometimes see those who were making recovery, through the barbed wire, clad in bandages and perhaps learning to walk again. We sometimes waved to them and they waved back. There were POW camps in the surrounding district, at Barnard Castle and Wolsingham and towards the end of the war, groups of POW's would be brought into Bishop on a Sunday, to attend Divine Worship. I shall never forget one Sunday morning when the captain and crew of a captured German U-Boat came to Wesley Chapel, to the morning service. They were under escort by the army of course, but most had no desire to escape. Where could they go, most had lost their homes and families so my dad learned. That morning our minister included some Lutheran hymns in the service and the lesson was read in German, by Dr Wise, who taught that language at the local grammar school.

They were not the monsters that I expected, but ordinary men, just like our dads. No doubt, they would be thinking of their own families as they sang those familiar hymns, wondering if they would ever see them again.

CHAPTER 25

DANCE ON JOSSIE

Arnie came running up to our house one morning to tell us that his dad had arrived home. He had been dropped off by an army lorry during the night, following a telegram just a few hours earlier. This was great news and Arnie was so excited, hadn't seen his dad for five years, although an occasional letter did get through from the POW camp in Germany. Mr Golledge had been captured early in the war, on the retreat to Dunkirk and spent the war in a prisoner of war camp, until his release. He had been an amateur athlete before the war and quite a good boxer. So there was great rejoicing when the Golledges' dad arrived home. Arnie blurted it all out. "Yer should see what me dad's brought back, a German helmet, a Hitler Youth dagger and lots of cigarettes." Besides his kit bag he had a suitcase bulging with cigarettes. Later, Arnie managed to pinch a packet, there were so many, they'd never be missed. These were Royalty King Size, previously unknown to us. How we puffed them later over the water tower, I made myself sick. The odd Woodbine, or Capstan, I could manage, but Royalty King Size were way beyond me. I only tried one, that was the finish.

Mr Golledge was a very nice man, I thought, full of fun, I suppose he was so thrilled to be back home. At that time

Joe Louis was the world heavyweight boxing champion. Mr Golledge would spar up to me in his vest, as he shaved in their scullery. "Come on then, get yer fists up," as he danced around me. "Bah, yer know what Brian, you'd make a good boxer, yer've got the right build. In fact yer look a lot like Joe Louis." That was a great compliment to me and made me feel proud. On reflection I suppose it was true, my hair was usually tousled and fuzzy and my face often black.

I don't think that Arnie's dad had been badly treated in the POW camp, not like those in concentration camps, but he had no time at all for Germans. He was so glad to be home and never wanted to see another German in his life.

It was a Saturday morning. That was great, no school. I would lie in bed sometimes and hear the butcher's cart come crunching up the street. The commands to the horse, "Come on boy, come on boy, steady now – whoa now." Billy the store butcher would open the front door and shout. "Butcher love. Ar've got yer a nice bit of sirloin today pet". Then my mam would go out to the cart. That morning remains forever in my memory, it must have been early, before the butcher came. My mam came rushing up the stairs, the bedroom door was thrust open. There was urgency in her step, just like when she used to come up to scold me for frightening Bette. Her voice was excited, as she shouted out her news. "Brian – Hitler's dead, they've just given it out on the wireless".

This was the best news I had ever heard in my life. I felt a warm glow of pleasure surging through me. This would mean that the war would soon be over, what rapture. There would be bananas again and as many sweets as I could eat. I was so excited and was soon dressed and out in the street, I'd forgotten to wash, what did it matter. Then a loud voice from our front door, "Brian", shouted my mam, "come back in here and get your face washed. Fancy goin' out like that, straight from bed." She soon hauled me into the scullery and made me have a good wash. "Don't forget your neck," she reminded me, as she always did, "Ar want to see no tide mark."

I soon passed muster and was on my way to call for my my mates. Everyone was buoyant with the news and knew that the end of the war couldn't be far off. The date for VE Day, was announced. The days that were to follow were full of buzz and excitement. We learned that there were to be street parties and bonfires throughout the land. There were lots of preparations to be made and as lads, the centre of our focus was the bonfire. This would be bigger and hotter than any Gunpowder Plot bonfire and our Hitler would make a, 'Nice Guy'. I felt warm and happy with anticipation, as I imagined our massive bonfire, scorching and crackling up the water tower wall, sending sparks and smoke into the sky.

I must have dozed off – Arnie was shaking me. "Bah Joss, yer've let yer taties burn, there's nowt left." It was true, I opened my eyes and looked down into the glowing white embers. My spuds were like lumps of coal, burnt to cinders. I began to feel the imprint of the milk crate on my backside, through the thin layer of sacking, as I eased myself forward from my slouched position against the school railings.

The other lads had gone, apart from Arnie, who was just finishing off a Royalty King Size. "Want a puff, Joss?" Eyeing the fat dump with suspicion, I shook my head, and wandered back into the street. The music was still playing and some people were dancing. I gazed in wonder and joy at the string of coloured lights against the starry sky and felt so good to be alive, what a lucky lad I was.

Sergeant Dexter's girl was there. "How about a dance Jossie?" I'd never danced in my life, didn't know the first thing about it. But thought, why not? – Dance on Jossie, after all, it's not every day that we win the war!.

—— **End** ——

GLOSSARY

Ack-Ack – anti-aircraft gun
Ar – I
ard – old
bairn – child
bank – surface
bank head – structure & wheel above pit shaft
blaring – crying
bool – bowl
boodie – porcelain
brazant – brazen
bullet – boiled sweet
bunch – kick or strike
caller – fresh
canny – cute or nice
champion – just the job
clarts – mud
crack – talk
crowdie – hen meal
dar – dad
draw – brew
dyke – hedge
fatha – farther
fond – simple
gadgie – man
gan – go
giz – give us
gully – large knife
hacky – dirty
howay – come on
howi – come on
hoy – throw
hunkers – haunches
knar – know
laden tin – large tin can with handle
loosed – released
marrer – work mate in the pit
mast – brewed
muggles – marbles
nettie – outside earth toilet
out bye – towards the shaft
ower – over
ower't – over the
plodge – paddle
progger – tool for clipping mat making
seest tha – you see
shig – share
spuggie – sparrow
styth – smoke or fumes
tak – take
t'ard – the old
the – you
thi – thy or your
thoo – you
tit – to the
torn – turn
tout – rope
we's – who is
wowie – treacle